AMERICAN LIFE
IN THE 1970s

70s

BY SUE BRADFORD EDWARDS

CONTENT CONSULTANT
Benjamin Waterhouse, PhD
Associate Professor, History
University of North Carolina at Chapel Hill

ICONIC AMERICAN DECADES

Essential Library

An Imprint of Abdo Publishing
abdobooks.com

ABDOBOOKS.COM

Published by Abdo Publishing, a division of ABDO, PO Box 398166, Minneapolis, Minnesota 55439. Copyright © 2024 by Abdo Consulting Group, Inc. International copyrights reserved in all countries. No part of this book may be reproduced in any form without written permission from the publisher. Essential Library™ is a trademark and logo of Abdo Publishing.

Printed in the United States of America, North Mankato, Minnesota.
052023
092023

Cover Photos: NASA (rocket); Charles Tasnadi/AP Images (Washington Monument); Tony Tomsic/AP Images (Hank Aaron); SSPL/Getty Images (Speak & Spell); Selyutina Olga/Shutterstock Images (disco ball [back]); Radik Khuzin/Shutterstock Images (oil pump); AP Images (Richard Nixon); Shutterstock Images (skateboard, power plant); Everett Collection/Shutterstock Images (planes [back], no gas sign); Zubkova Iuliia/Shutterstock Images (pattern)
Interior Photos: Howard Ruffner/Archive Photos/Getty Images, 4–5; Bettmann/Getty Images, 6, 9, 27, 28–29, 100 (bottom); Universal History Archive/Universal Images Group/Getty Images, 10–11; Watford/Mirrorpix/Getty Images, 14–15; Shutterstock Images, 16, 40, 99; Warren M. Winterbottom/AP Images, 18; Barry Sweet/AP Images, 20–21; Jim Wells/AP Images, 23, 31; Charles Tasnadi/AP Images, 24–25, 100 (top); Pictorial Press Ltd/Alamy, 33; AP Images, 36–37, 39, 44–45, 67, 68–69, 80–81, 84, 101 (left), 101 (right); William Karel/Gamma-Rapho/Getty Images, 41; NASA/AP Images, 46–47; NASA, 48–49; SSPL/Getty Images, 51, 102 (bottom); William Berry/Atlanta Journal-Constitution/AP Images, 52; Trong Nguyen/Shutterstock Images, 54–55; Barry Thumma/AP Images, 57, 103 (right); Chris Walter/WireImage/Getty Images, 58–59; Michael Ochs Archives/Stringer/Getty Images, 60–61, 74; David Redfern/Redferns/Getty Images, 62; Edson Garcia/Shutterstock Images, 63, 102 (top); George Sheldon/Shutterstock Images, 65; Doreen Spooner/Mirrorpix/Getty Images, 71; RGR Collection/Alamy, 73; Heritage Art/Heritage Images/Hulton Archive/Getty Images, 77; Tony Tomsic/AP Images, 78–79; Robyn Mackenzie/Shutterstock Images, 82; Rich Clarkson/Rich Clarkson and Assoc./NCAA Photos/Getty Images, 87; Mark Duncan/AP Images, 88–89; Jeff Glidden/AP Images, 90; YES Market Media/Shutterstock Images, 92–93; Richard Shotwell/Invision/AP Images, 94–95; Luqman Abu Hassan/Shutterstock Images, 96, 103 (left)

Editor: Alyssa Sorenson
Series Designer: Maggie Villaume

Library of Congress Control Number: 2021951578

PUBLISHER'S CATALOGING-IN-PUBLICATION DATA

Names: Edwards, Sue Bradford, author.
Title: American life in the 1970s / by Sue Bradford Edwards
Description: Minneapolis, Minnesota: Abdo Publishing, 2024 | Series: Iconic American decades | Includes online resources and index.
Identifiers: ISBN 9781532198069 (lib. bdg.) | ISBN 9781098271718 (ebook)
Subjects: LCSH: Nineteen seventies--Juvenile literature. | United States--History--Juvenile literature. | Civilization, Modern--20th century--Juvenile literature.
Classification: DDC 973.92--dc23

CONTENTS

Students who gathered to protest at Kent State didn't know they would be part of a tragic and historic event.

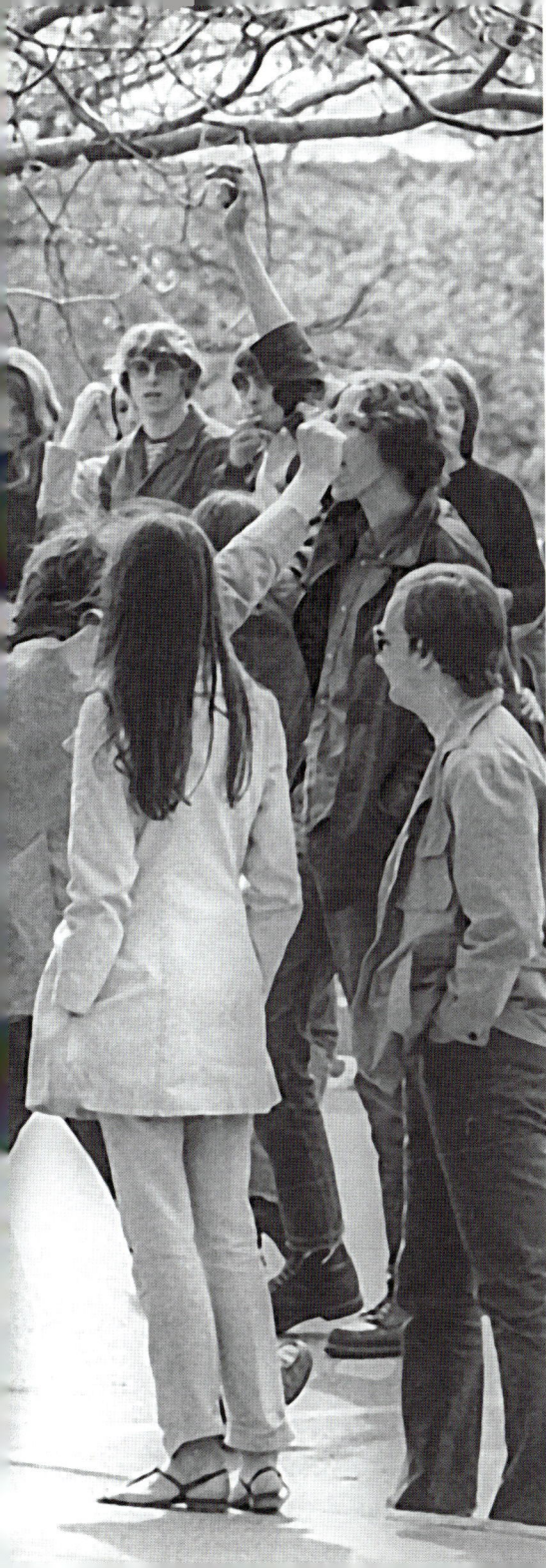

CHAPTER ONE

KENT STATE

At 11:00 a.m. on May 4, 1970, a group of unarmed students gathered at Kent State University in Kent, Ohio. An anti-war rally protesting the Vietnam War (1954–1975) had been scheduled for noon. Approximately 3,000 people had gathered as the time for the rally approached.[1]

No one knows exactly how many people were there to actually protest, but the number is estimated at 500. They gathered around the Victory Bell at one end of the open area known as the Commons. Another 1,000 people were there to support the protesters, cheering them on. Approximately 1,500 more were there to see what would happen. Across the Commons from the protesters were 100 National Guardsmen, who had been sent there by

Guardsmen tried to get protesters to leave by throwing tear gas, but many students were determined to stay.

the Ohio governor to maintain order.[2] The rally had been scheduled to protest the war, but many protesters focused their objections on the soldiers present on campus.

Shortly before noon, General Robert Canterbury made the decision to cancel the demonstration. Canterbury was the highest-ranking guardsman present. At his order, a campus police officer used a bullhorn to tell everyone to leave. When this had no effect, the officer and several guardsmen in a jeep drove around the Commons. When the protesters were told to disperse, they shouted back, and some of them threw rocks.

Canterbury commanded his men to load their weapons. Tear gas was fired into the crowd around the Victory Bell, but it was a windy day, so the tear gas had no effect. As the guardsmen marched forward to disperse the crowd, some people moved out of the Commons and into a parking lot. Others moved downhill onto a practice football field.

Most of the guardsmen followed the group onto the football field. The rock-throwing continued, and people shouted at the soldiers. The guardsmen drew together and some knelt, aiming their guns at the crowd, but no shots were fired.

DISSATISFACTION WITH THE WAR

Between 1965 and 1973, the Gallup polling organization surveyed a number of people to get their views on the Vietnam War. In August 1965, people who were 50 and older were more likely than people under age 30 to say that it was a mistake to get the United States involved in Vietnam. In 1973, older people continued to have this view, with 69 percent surveyed saying that Vietnam was a mistake compared to 53 percent of younger people with this view.[3]

The guardsmen retreated back up the hill toward the Commons. When they reached the hilltop, approximately 70 of the soldiers turned and fired into the crowd. Four students were killed. Another nine were seriously injured.[4] The event became known as the Kent State massacre.

Photography student John Filo snapped a roll of pictures. He remembered thinking that no one would believe soldiers were firing on students in the United States. One of his photographs, of a girl kneeling beside the lifeless body of a student, was used in newspapers and magazines across the country. The photo won the Pulitzer Prize the following year.

WAR AND PROTESTS

The US military escalated its involvement in Vietnam in 1965. People in support of the conflict said the United States' involvement was essential to fighting the larger war against communism. US leaders wanted to keep communism from spreading around the world. At this time, Vietnam had been divided into two parts. The North was ruled by the Vietnamese Communist Party, which was led by Ho Chi Minh and was backed by China and the Soviet Union. South Vietnam had a Western-leaning government and had support from the United States and some Western

European countries. North Vietnam wanted to unify the country under communist rule, and leaders in the United States wanted to prevent this from happening. By 1969, approximately 500,000 US military personnel were stationed in Vietnam.[5]

Some people disliked the United States' involvement in Vietnam and spoke out about it. One protest happened on April 1, 1965. Held on the University of Wisconsin, Madison, campus, this teach-in protest was organized so that students could gather together and learn about the war.

It was often students who were vocal in speaking out against the war. This was especially the case after 1966, when changes to the draft made it possible to draft male college students if their grades weren't

JACKSON STATE COLLEGE

The tragedy at Jackson State College, a historically Black college, in 1970 was a result of growing racial tension between the students and law enforcement. Tensions escalated on May 15, 1970, when rumors circulated that a local civil rights leader and his wife had been killed. A protester not connected to the college set a dump truck on fire. Though this hardly posed a threat, the police officers brought their assault weapons onto the campus. After the fire was doused, the officers advanced to Alexander Hall, a women's dormitory, claiming that there was a sniper in the dorm. Some students in front of the dorm threw bricks and rocks at the officers, and the police responded by opening fire. More than 150 rounds were fired into the building, which still bore the bullet marks decades later. Two students were killed in the gunfire and another 12 were injured, but the story did not make national news.[6]

good enough. Many of these students had friends, relatives, and classmates who were dying overseas too.

During his presidential campaign in 1968, President Richard Nixon promised to end the Vietnam War. This contributed to his election win in 1968. However, the war continued during his presidency. On April 30, 1970, Nixon announced that the Vietnam War had been expanded

After the guardsmen lined up and opened fired on students, people across the nation debated whether their actions were justifiable.

into the neighboring country of Cambodia. Attacks on locations in Cambodia started on April 29. Communist South Vietnamese soldiers known as the Vietcong had been storing weapons in Cambodia. By entering this country, the Vietcong could rearm and regroup, avoiding US forces.

Nixon's Cambodia announcement led to protests like the one at Kent State. After the massacre, even more protests occurred. In the weeks that followed the shooting, more than 1,300 demonstrations took place, and 500 campuses were closed due to the unrest and violence.[7] Investigators looked into the events at Kent State as people across the United States demanded accountability.

INVESTIGATION

Investigations into what occurred at Kent State revealed few answers. Canterbury believed that he was in charge because he thought a state of emergency had been declared. The day before the shooting, Ohio governor James Rhodes flew to Kent. At a press conference, he said he would seek a court order to declare a state of emergency because of both the protests in town and those on the college campus. In town, protesters built bonfires in the streets, blocked traffic, and broke shop windows. On campus, a building burned. But Rhodes never declared a state of emergency. If he had, Canterbury would have been in charge.

The guardsmen said they fired because they felt threatened and feared for their lives. They were outnumbered by rock-throwing students. But the closest student who was shot was 60 feet (18 m) away and the farthest student was 750 feet (230 m) away from the soldiers. Eight of the guardsmen were charged and tried in 1974, but Judge Frank Battisti dismissed all charges, saying that the case against them was too weak to go to trial.

A presidential commission known as the Scranton Commission was established in June 1971 to investigate the shootings. This investigation reported, "The indiscriminate firing of rifles into a crowd of students and the deaths that followed were unnecessary, unwarranted, and inexcusable."[8]

The guardsmen may not have been convicted, but some Americans viewed them as guilty nonetheless. At the same time, there were some people who viewed the shootings as justified. They said the guardsmen were defending themselves against a rowdy crowd.

THE 1970s

Angus Johnston is a historian from the City University of New York. He studies student activism. In 2020, he told an NBC News reporter that Kent State was a turning point in the United States. "It was definitely understood very quickly as an indication that things in the US—on and off campus—were spiraling out of control," said Johnston.[9]

> **"THE ME DECADE"**
>
> Journalist Tom Wolfe nicknamed the 1970s "The Me Decade." He said young people had access to many things compared to earlier generations, and they wanted these things all for themselves—consumer goods, freedom, and individualism. He believed that young people in the 1970s saw that they could have more and had no problem demanding it for themselves.

The decades leading up to the 1970s, and the decade itself, were marked by political protests. People protested against the continued Vietnam War. There were also demonstrations for equal rights for women, American Indian rights, and environmental protection.

The population was more urban than ever while simultaneously becoming more diverse. New technologies, such as video games, were becoming widely available, and a growing number of homes had access to them. It was a decade of great change throughout the United States.

In the 1970s, Chicago, Illinois, was one of the busiest cities in the country.

CHAPTER TWO

AMERICANS OF THE 1970s

In the 1790s, the United States was a new nation that was very rural. Although there were cities, most people lived on small farms or in small towns. By the late 1800s, the numbers of people living in the northern cities had started to grow. A large part of the population growth was due to global immigration. Additionally, people in rural areas were moving to the cities because of the growing need for workers in northern and midwestern factories.

By 1970, only 25 percent of the US population lived in rural areas, but there were regional variations. For example, in the southern United States, 33 percent of the population lived in rural areas. There were also nine US states in which the majority of the population was rural: Vermont, West Virginia,

North and South Dakota, North and South Carolina, Mississippi, Arkansas, and Alaska.[1]

During the 1970s, the United States continued to grow still more urban, but the majority of new development was no longer in the industrial north. Instead, growth occurred in the southern and southwestern areas, known as the Sun Belt, where the US oil industry and mining were developing. As these industries grew, people moved south to take advantage of the jobs that were becoming available there.

CITY LIVING

In 1970, the four largest US cities were, starting with the largest, New York City; Chicago, Illinois; Los Angeles, California; and Philadelphia, Pennsylvania. That year, the population of New York City was 7,894,862 people.[2] During this decade it was a city in turmoil. The United States was experiencing an economic downturn that left many people out of work. Crime rates rose. Hundreds of thousands of people moved out of New York City to the suburbs, looking for jobs.

Chicago was the second-largest city in the United States in 1970, with a population of 3,366,957 people.[3] Like many large US cities in the 1970s, Chicago had a pollution problem, but it was still a vibrant city. During the week, city streets were crowded with cars as people drove to work. One popular Chicago event throughout the 1970s was the Bud Billiken Parade, an African American event first held in 1929. In the 1970s, marching bands and floats went down the street, and families gathered together to barbecue and listen to live music.

In 1970, Los Angeles was the third-largest city in the United States, with a population of 2,816,061 people.[4] Similar to other cities, pollution was a problem. In Los Angeles, the most obvious sign of this was the smog that darkened the air. The city was known for an easygoing attitude paired with the glitz and glamour of the entertainment industry.

The fourth-largest city in the United States in 1970 was Philadelphia, with a population of 1,948,609 people.[5] Pollution and poverty were evident in the city. But the city also had beautiful architecture and cultural treasures such as the Philadelphia Museum of Art.

POPULATION BY RACE

In 1970, approximately 203.2 million people lived in the United States.[6] The racial makeup was 87.4 percent white,

FEAR CITY

In the 1970s, New York City was nicknamed "Fear City" because of its high crime rate. Between 1960 and 1970, the homicide rate more than doubled. Muggings, gang violence, subway crimes, car thefts, burglaries, and rapes also increased. It wasn't until the 1990s that crime rates began to drop.

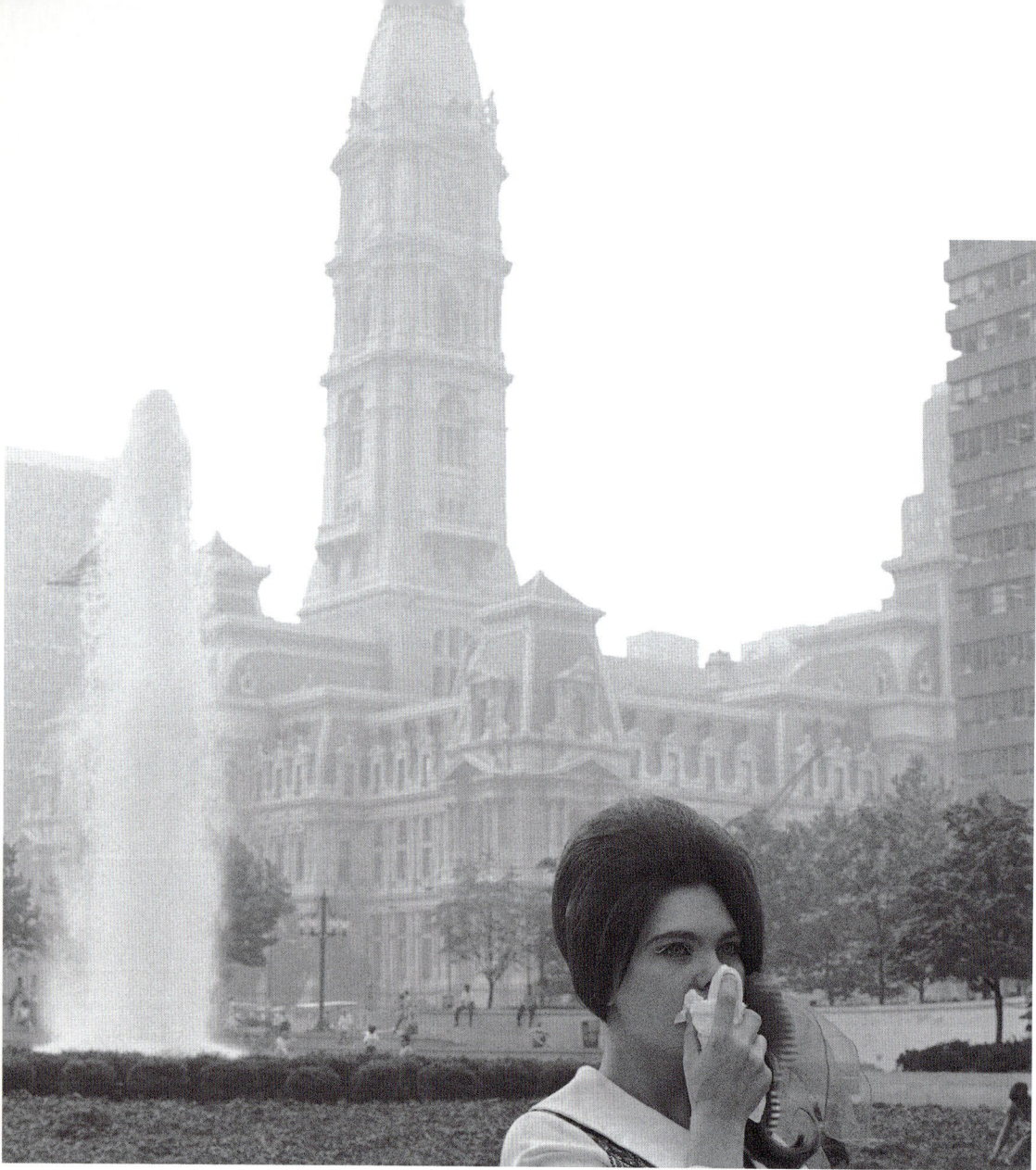

In the 1970s, haze from air pollution in Philadelphia lowered air quality and posed health risks.

11.1 percent Black, and 1.4 percent people of other races, but the composition of this population was changing. By 1980, the population of the United States rose to 226.5 million people. Of these people, 83.2 percent were white, 11.7 percent were African American, and 5.2 percent were people of other races.[7]

Part of this shift was due to changes in immigration law that impacted who could enter the United States. From 1920 to 1960, immigration had been low, especially during World War II (1939–1945). Then the Immigration and Nationality Act of 1965 passed, reducing restrictions based on a potential immigrant's country of origin. While previous laws had favored Western European immigrants, the new law gave priority to skilled immigrants such as doctors, engineers, lawyers, teachers, architects, and people who already had family members living in the United States. These revised policies allowed new groups to enter the United States.

In 1975, Congress passed the Indochina Migration and Refugee Assistance Act. This

AMERASIAN CHILDREN

During the time that the US military was in Vietnam, US servicemen there had thousands of children with Vietnamese women. These children became known as Amerasian children. When the United States withdrew from Vietnam, many mothers worried for their children's safety. Some women left their children at orphanages or even dropped them into trash cans. In 1987, Congress passed the Amerasian Homecoming Act to help these people immigrate to the United States with their families. Some had letters or photos that could prove the required link to the United States, but many items had been destroyed by frightened mothers. Today, DNA tests can prove if people have family members, such as fathers or half-siblings, living in the United States.

allowed people fleeing from war and its aftermath in Vietnam, Laos, and Cambodia to more easily enter the United States. Roughly 130,000 refugees entered the United States because of this law.[8] Some of these people had helped the US military during the war.

During the 1970s, the United States admitted hundreds of thousands of immigrants each year. Changes in immigration law meant that more immigrants were arriving from Asia and Latin America. Slowly, this shifted the racial and ethnic makeup of the nation's population.

INCOME, GENDER, AND RACE IN EMPLOYMENT

In 1970, Congress increased the minimum wage from $1.30 to $1.45. By 1979, it had gone up to $2.90.[9] The overall median annual income in 1970 was $9,870, meaning half of all households made more than this amount and half made less. When only nonwhite families are considered, the median household income dropped to $6,520.[10]

In the 1960s, the number of men working year-round increased, and the gap between the number of working white men and working Black men decreased. These improvements are believed to have been the result of an economic boom in the 1960s and an increase in educational

In 1970, people lined up at the State Employment Security Department in Seattle, Washington, to get unemployment checks.

opportunities for Black Americans. However, these employment trends did not hold into the 1970s. Instead, the number of men working year-round dropped, and the number of unemployed men increased. The employment gap between white and Black men also increased.

At the same time, an adjustment was happening in the workforce. In the 1970s, baby boomers—people born between 1946 and 1964—were entering the labor market in large numbers. In addition, a growing number of women were also seeking jobs. Both of these trends led to increased competition for jobs in the 1970s.

The 1970s were also a time of economic difficulties. Inflation meant that the cost of products was going up, but the number of jobs was not growing. People had a hard time paying higher prices for goods and services.

The economic problems weighed more heavily on Black workers than on white workers. Although there were more educational opportunities for Black Americans than before, there were still many people who could not afford an advanced education. Without the training this education provided, these people were often the ones who could not find work.

The Bureau of the Census reported that in 1970,

CHANGES IN THE 1970 CENSUS

Periodically, the government changes what data is collected in the census, an official count of the US population complete with details on each individual. In 1970, the secretary of commerce, the cabinet official in charge of the census, added a question about Hispanic origin. People filling out the census were asked for the first time if they came from or were descended from someone who came from Mexico, Cuba, Puerto Rico, Central America, or South America, or someone who had a Spanish background.

Millions of people lived in low-income areas in New York City in 1970.

approximately 25.5 million people, or 13 percent of the overall population, lived in poverty. But the rates differed significantly between races. The poverty rate for Black people was approximately three times higher than the rate for white people.[11]

Protesters in Washington, DC, demonstrate against the Vietnam War.

CHAPTER THREE

POLITICS OF THE 1970s

Politically, the 1970s were a tumultuous time. When the decade started, the United States was still involved in the Vietnam War. Protests were held for numerous reasons, including objections to the draft. In the draft, eligible men were assigned a number based on their birth date. Draft boards would request groups of men to get evaluated and see if they were fit to serve in the military.

Many people protested the draft. Some men burned their draft cards or never registered, which they were supposed to do when they turned 18. Others registered as conscientious objectors and were given noncombat roles when drafted. Still other men failed to report when their number was called up, claimed that they were physically unable to fight, or fled to Canada.

So many people had fled to Canada that after the war ended, President Jimmy Carter pardoned the draft offenders and allowed them to return to the United States.

One Vietnam War protest was the May Day protest of 1971. Its slogan was "If the government won't stop the war, we'll stop the government."[1] Protesters planned to shut down Washington, DC, by disrupting the flow of traffic. On the morning of May 3, tens of thousands of protesters entered the city and blocked streets with wooden barricades and parked cars. President Richard Nixon had heard about their plans and had police, soldiers, and National Guardsmen on hand. Thousands of people were arrested but few were officially charged. The protest stopped traffic for only a few hours.

AMERICAN BICENTENNIAL

Between April 1975 and July 1976, events were held across the United States to celebrate the country's 200th birthday, known as the American Bicentennial. One event featuring President Gerald Ford occurred on April 18, 1975. The president went to Old North Church in Boston, Massachusetts, where two lanterns had signaled to patriot Paul Revere the route that the British Army was taking during the American Revolutionary War (1775–1783). Ford lit a third lantern to signal that the United States was moving into a third century. Throughout the celebrations, Americans bought and collected an array of commemorative items, including specially minted bicentennial quarters, flags, clothing, and more.

FIGHTING FOR RIGHTS

Protests during the 1970s weren't only about the Vietnam War. In 1968, the American Indian Movement (AIM) was founded. The organization's leaders worked to improve the lives of Native peoples. The group demanded that

While some people burned their draft cards as a form of protest, others believed actions like these were disloyal to the United States.

the government follow through on its promises made in various treaties with American Indian groups. These treaties were signed in the 1700s and 1800s. In the treaties, the government recognized that certain land belonged to American Indian tribes and nations. In spite of these treaties, state and federal governments took treaty lands for white settlement.

In November 1969, AIM and several other groups worked together to seize Alcatraz Island in San Francisco Bay, the site of a closed prison, to protest the seizure of Native lands by the US government decades earlier. The groups demanded the government give them the deed to the island and set up a Native university and cultural center. Many of the original occupiers were university students who returned to classes in January 1970. Other groups of people, including non–American Indians, came to the island, lived there temporarily, then left. On June 10, 1971, armed federal marshals, agents from the Federal Bureau of Investigation (FBI), and other police officers swept in and removed the rest of the unarmed occupiers. The occupation inspired future protests for Native rights.

Women also worked for equality, and in 1972 Congress passed the Equal Rights Amendment (ERA) and sent it to the states for ratification. The proposed constitutional amendment stated that equal rights would not be denied because of a person's sex, that Congress would enforce

In 1978, a group of American Indians marched from San Francisco to Washington, DC, to protest legislation that threatened American Indian rights. It took them five months to reach the US capital.

the law, and that it would go into effect two years after the final state approved it. Many people demonstrated in support of the amendment. A lot of women wanted equal job and educational opportunities, but others feared the changes the amendment would bring and protested against it.

Among the women who did not support the ERA was conservative attorney Phyllis Schlafly. She believed that the passage of the ERA would endanger women and families. Schlafly reminded people that if the ERA passed, her daughters and other young women could be drafted and sent to war. Thirty-eight states were needed to make the amendment a law, but not all supported it within the given deadline set by Congress. The ERA was not added to the Constitution.

Women also fought for rights over what happens to their bodies. In 1970, a group of people filed a class-action lawsuit saying that states should not be able to prevent women from getting abortions. The case, known as *Roe v. Wade*, went all the way to the US Supreme Court. On January 22, 1973, the Supreme Court stated that restrictive state laws regarding abortion were unconstitutional because they invaded a woman's right to privacy. However, in 2022 the US Supreme Court reversed its decision and overturned *Roe v. Wade*. This allowed states to make their own restrictive abortion laws.

WATERGATE

Another volatile political event during this decade was the Watergate scandal. On June 17, 1972, during Nixon's campaign for reelection, a break-in occurred at the Washington, DC, offices of the Democratic National Committee in the Watergate Hotel and Office Complex. Police caught

GLORIA
STEINEM

Gloria Steinem graduated from college in 1956 and studied in India for two years. Back in the United States, Steinem worked as a journalist. She was frustrated that most women in publishing were given research or secretary work, leaving the writing to men. Steinem's first stories were about fashion, but she continued to push for other types of assignments.

In 1971, Steinem founded a magazine called *Ms.* with journalists Patricia Carbine and Letty Cottin Pogrebin. The trio was disappointed in other women's magazines that avoided politics and instead focused on clothing and cooking. Although *Ms.* was initially an insert in *New York* magazine, by 1972 it had gained enough popularity to be published independently. Steinem worked as an editor and writer for the magazine for the next 15 years.

In 1972, Steinem worked with Congresswomen Bella Abzug and Shirley Chisholm, along with feminist Betty Friedan, to form the National Women's Political Caucus. This group worked for gender equality and to support the political campaigns of women who supported equality. In 2013, Steinem was awarded the Presidential Medal of Freedom by President Barack Obama. This is the highest award given to civilians in the United States.

Gloria Steinem stood up for her beliefs and was a vocal member of the women's liberation movement.

and arrested five men, including James W. McCord Jr.—the security chief of a group called the Committee to Re-elect the President. The arrests were reported the next morning by the *Washington Post*.

Nixon said he knew nothing of the burglary, but the FBI and two *Washington Post* reporters, Carl Bernstein and Bob Woodward, kept digging. A secret FBI informant relayed information to the reporters, who wrote an article revealing that Nixon had known about the break-in and his campaign had financed it. Still, Nixon won reelection in 1972.

When the White House investigated the Watergate incident, it claimed that no connections were found to anyone employed by the White House. Meanwhile, the five burglars had gone to trial, and the judge found links to multiple Nixon staffers. After being ordered to hand over several taped conversations, Nixon turned over some edited tapes and failed to surrender others. As evidence mounted that Nixon had known about the burglaries and that he had ordered the Central Intelligence Agency to interfere with the

NIXON IMPEACHMENT

The US Constitution states that the House of Representatives can charge any federal official with treason, bribery, or other crimes. Then the Senate tries the case. The House Judiciary Committee's hearing to impeach Nixon because of the Watergate scandal started in May 1974. Afterward, the House Judiciary Committee charged Nixon with abuse of power and obstruction of justice for interfering in the Watergate investigations. Nixon resigned before the House voted on whether to impeach him. Nixon did not admit guilt but said he no longer had enough support to effectively serve as president.

During the Watergate scandal, President Nixon continued to maintain his innocence.

FBI's investigation, the House of Representatives investigated Nixon for possible impeachment. Rather than face the charges, he resigned on August 8, 1974. Vice President Gerald Ford assumed the presidency and pardoned Nixon.

Ford sought to heal divisions caused by the Vietnam War. In September 1974, he offered amnesty to draft dodgers who had fled to Canada or deserted during active service. This decision angered veterans and their families. In their own form of protest, some veterans sent Ford the service medals they earned during war. In 1976, Ford lost the presidential election to Jimmy Carter.

ENVIRONMENT AND ENERGY

Energy and the environment were both important topics to Americans in the 1970s, in part because industrialization in preceding decades had polluted both urban and natural landscapes. In January 1969, an oil rig off the coast of Santa Barbara, California, leaked millions of barrels of oil into the ocean. In June, the Cuyahoga River in Cleveland, Ohio, caught fire when oil and other pollutants in the water ignited. This was the same year Americans learned their national symbol, the bald eagle, was endangered because of the chemical pesticide DDT.

These events made people more aware of the damage being done to the environment. Wisconsin senator Gaylord Nelson organized an event on April 22, 1970, to educate people across the country about environmental issues. An estimated 10 percent of the US population participated, including more than 2,000 colleges and universities and 10,000 public schools.[2] This event was the first Earth Day. It encouraged politicians to support legislation that would fight pollution and address other environmental issues.

Nixon created the Council on Environmental Quality in 1970 to help protect the environment. The council recommended that existing government responsibilities be consolidated into one agency

that could research problems, set standards, enforce air and water pollution regulations, and more. William Ruckelshaus, the first director of this new Environmental Protection Agency, was sworn in on December 4, 1970.

Another new government department was created under President Jimmy Carter. This one involved energy. In 1973, Arab states organized an embargo, refusing to export oil to the United States because of the latter's support of Israel. Americans worried about energy. When Carter took office in 1977, an unusually severe winter led to natural gas shortages, closing both factories and schools. To address the growing energy issues, Carter wanted to create a department that would be in charge of the country's energy plan and look into the development of new energy technology. In 1977, Carter signed the Department of Energy Organization Act, which consolidated 30 energy-related functions within a single department: the US Department of Energy.

President Nixon's 1972 trip to China lasted a week.

CHAPTER FOUR

WAR AND CONFLICT OF THE 1970s

The Cold War (1947–1991) was a political conflict that started after World War II and lasted until 1991. It pitted the United States and its ally nations against the Soviet Union, China, and their allies. President Richard Nixon worked to reduce tensions between the United States and other countries.

On July 15, 1971, Nixon announced on live television that he would visit China. He had been invited by Chinese premier Zhou Enlai to open relations between the two countries. The timing wasn't coincidental, because relations between China and the Soviet Union had worsened. China still opposed

COLD WAR

The Cold War sprang up due to the conflicting beliefs of the United States and the Soviet Union. Although the two countries never had direct military confrontation with each other, they did engage in proxy wars. These conflicts happen when third parties intervene in another country's war in order to push a favorable outcome. The Vietnam War was an example of a proxy war between the United States and the Soviet Union. In addition, during the Cold War, trade, relations, and travel were limited between the two sides. The conflict ended when the Soviet Union collapsed in 1991 after the Soviet president allowed the country's republics to become independent.

many US policies, but during Nixon's February 1972 visit, anti-US slogans and chants were curtailed and well-dressed citizens were stationed along the Great Wall to look like tourists and make a good impression. The visit didn't solve every problem between the two countries, but it did open the possibility of talks and future cooperative efforts.

In May 1972, Nixon visited the Soviet Union, traveling to the capital city of Moscow. This was an official summit, and Nixon worked with Soviet leader Leonid Brezhnev to create new policies. One of the agreements reached by Nixon and Brezhnev laid the groundwork for a joint 1975 space flight, with the two nations cooperating instead of competing. Additionally, the Strategic Arms Limitations Treaty limited the size of each side's nuclear arsenal. These visits helped to reduce tensions between the United States and both China and the Soviet Union.

THE END OF THE VIETNAM WAR

The United States had been in Vietnam starting in the 1950s. At that time, North Vietnam, supported by communist China, wanted to unify the country under communist rule. South Vietnam

RICHARD NIXON

Richard Nixon served in the US Navy during World War II. In 1947, he joined the US House of Representatives, and in later years he went to the Senate, representing California. He then served as vice president from 1953 to 1961 under President Dwight D. Eisenhower.

As president, Nixon wanted to reduce the conflicts that ensnared the United States and set about reconciling the country with various foreign powers. This led to his 1972 visits to China and the Soviet Union. He was able to ease some of the tensions with these two powers, and he was also able to reduce the numbers of nuclear weapons held by the United States and the Soviet Union.

Following the Watergate scandal and his 1974 resignation as president, Nixon and his wife retired to their San Clemente, California, home. Nixon wrote several books on foreign policy, as well as *RN: The Memoir of Richard Nixon*, which was published in 1978. Nixon traveled worldwide, sometimes meeting with world leaders. In 1991, he traveled to the Soviet Union and advocated for the United States to support the movement of former Soviet nations toward democracy and economic freedom.

Richard Nixon was the only president to ever resign.

fought to preserve a country allied with the United States. US politicians saw Vietnam as an opportunity to stand against communism. The United States was a staunch opponent of communism and didn't want it to spread around the globe. Upon taking office in 1961, President John F. Kennedy continued to support South Vietnam, sending aid and advisors. In 1965, as the communists gained ground in the south, President Lyndon B. Johnson initiated a bombing campaign in the north and sent in US troops. Nixon continued this policy during his presidency.

In 1973, Congress voted that no more US military operations would take place in Vietnam. In March 1975, the North Vietnamese army moved south. On April 30, 1975, the United States airlifted out the last members of its military, and the South Vietnamese government surrendered to the North.

OLD ENOUGH TO FIGHT, OLD ENOUGH TO VOTE

During World War II, Congress lowered the minimum draft age to 18. The slogan "old enough to fight, old enough to vote" was then used to advocate for lowering the voting age to 18. Michigan senator Arthur Vandenberg said in 1954, "They ought to be entitled to vote at 18 years of age for the kind of government for which they are best satisfied to fight."[1] Congress did not lower the voting age at that time, but the topic came up again during the Vietnam War. In 1971, the Twenty-sixth Amendment dropped the voting age to 18, extending the vote to ten million new voters.[2]

UNREST IN THE MIDDLE EAST

The Vietnam War wasn't the only military conflict to impact the United States during the 1970s. On October 6, 1973, Syria and Egypt both invaded Israel.

Israeli tanks pass through the desert during the Yom Kippur War.

The attacks took place on a Jewish holy day, Yom Kippur. Israeli forces were quickly pushed back. On October 19, Nixon announced a $2.2 billion aid package to Israel.[3] Because of help from the United States and other nations, Israel regrouped and pushed Syrian forces back, allowing Israel to enter Syrian territory. The Israeli Army also circled around the Egyptian forces by crossing the Suez Canal. Fighting in what came to be known as the Yom Kippur War ended on October 26.

That same month, Arab nations halted oil shipments to all countries, including the United States, that supported Israel in the Yom Kippur War. Gasoline prices in the United States increased and supplies were low. Gas station operators posted signs outside their businesses to let customers know when they ran out of gas. The US government stepped in, reducing speed limits so that cars burned less fuel and limiting the amount of gasoline that people could buy and when they could buy it. People panicked over shortages and sat in lines for hours to buy gasoline whenever they could. The embargo was finally lifted in March 1974.

In 1978, wishing to reduce war and global instability, President Jimmy Carter invited Israeli prime minister Menachem Begin and Egyptian president Anwar Sadat to Camp David, the presidential retreat in Maryland.

OIL CRISIS

The oil crisis impacted home heating, and Nixon encouraged people to adjust their thermostats. Nixon explained that if people dropped their home thermostats by four degrees Fahrenheit (2.2°C), the nation would save more than 400,000 barrels of heating oil each day. In order to set a good example, federal agencies dropped the thermostats in their buildings by four degrees.

The summit began on September 5 as Carter, Begin, and Sadat met without their foreign policy advisors. All went well for three days before the talks hit an impasse that was finally resolved on September 17, 1978. The leaders created a framework that they hoped would bring about peace in the Middle East, and Carter hoped this would encourage other Arab countries to join future peace talks. But rather than follow Egypt's lead, other Arab nations shunned Egypt.

THE HOSTAGE CRISIS

Another source of conflict stemmed from Iran. Mohammad Reza Shah Pahlavi, the shah of Iran, ruled this Middle Eastern nation from 1941 to 1979. He was a US ally who worked to modernize the nation, permitting women to vote and improving education. But students in Iran wanted democracy and a limit to his powers. In spite of food shortages, he held extravagant celebrations and lived luxuriously while also spending large sums of money to expand the military. Additionally, he used the US-trained secret police, the SAVAK, to silence his enemies. Islamic leaders led a revolution that removed him from power. On January 16, 1979, Pahlavi left Iran.

With the absence of Pahlavi, discontent focused on the United States, a nation that had supported him and Israel. On February 14, 1979, a group of Iranians attacked and briefly occupied the US Embassy in Iran. They killed several staff members and wounded others. The United States wanted to maintain the embassy, but it also wanted to minimize risk to its staff, so many people returned to the United States, reducing personnel from 1,400 to approximately 70.[4] On November 4, 1979, the US Embassy was attacked by approximately 3,000 Iranians who eventually

captured the embassy and 63 staff. Almost two weeks later, 13 of the hostages were released because the Iranians believed they were unlikely to be spies.[5]

On April 16, 1980, Carter approved an ambitious rescue plan that involved every branch of the US military, as well as Special Forces. The operation, which launched on April 24, failed after three helicopters were grounded and a dust storm limited visibility. After the mission was called off, one helicopter flew into a C-130 plane that carried fuel, killing multiple US soldiers. Carter's inability to bring the hostages home cost him politically. People sometimes saw the hostages on television with blindfolded eyes and tied hands while being paraded before Iranian crowds. The hostages were held for 444 days and released on January 20, 1981.

TIE A YELLOW RIBBON

In the early 1970s, songwriter L. Russell Brown read a story about a soldier returning from war. The soldier wrote his girlfriend a letter and told her to tie a yellow kerchief on a tree outside of town if she was interested in resuming their relationship. When the man reached the tree, it was covered in yellow handkerchiefs. With his partner Irwin Levine, Brown cowrote a song based on this folk tale. "Tie a Yellow Ribbon" became a hit in 1973. In December 1979, Penne Laingen, the wife of one of the Iranian hostages, remembered the song and suggested that yellow ribbons be tied on trees. The practice spread across the United States as a way for people to show their support for the hostages.

Armed Iranians searched hostages from the US Embassy in February 1979.

The space race pushed the United States to develop incredible technology and send astronauts to space.

CHAPTER FIVE

SCIENCE AND INVENTION IN THE 1970s

The space race between the United States and the Soviet Union started in the 1950s. It was another point of Cold War competition. The US government established the National Aeronautics and Space Administration (NASA) in 1958 to organize its efforts in space. In 1969, US astronauts Neil Armstrong and Buzz Aldrin become the first men to walk on the moon.

This space race continued into the 1970s. One of the decade's first missions was a near disaster for the United States. Apollo 13 was traveling to the moon in April 1970 when one of the spacecraft's oxygen tanks exploded. With help from mission control back on Earth, the three astronauts were able to survive and make it back home safely.

SALYUT

On April 19, 1971, the Soviet Union launched the world's first space station. Salyut was designed to operate in space for only six months. The three-man crew set a record with 24 continuous days in space, but when attempting to reenter the Earth's atmosphere, their craft depressurized and all three cosmonauts, the Russian term for astronauts, died. The Soviets continued to improve on the Salyut design, eventually launching seven versions of the Salyut space station.

A major milestone in US space exploration occurred on May 14, 1973, with the launch of Skylab, the first US space station. In a series of three missions, three-man crews lived and worked on the station. The first crew remained for 28 days, the second for 56 days, and the third for 84 days. Each mission set a US record for spaceflight duration. Crews conducted various tasks that involved observing the Sun and Earth from space and studying the effects of prolonged weightlessness on the human body.

In spite of the Cold War, the United States and the Soviet Union collaborated. In 1972, the two countries planned a joint mission to show that the two space programs could work together, and in 1975, that mission was a success when a US spacecraft docked with a Russian one. It opened the door for future cooperation, testing the compatibility of

Russian cosmonauts and US astronauts worked together while in space.

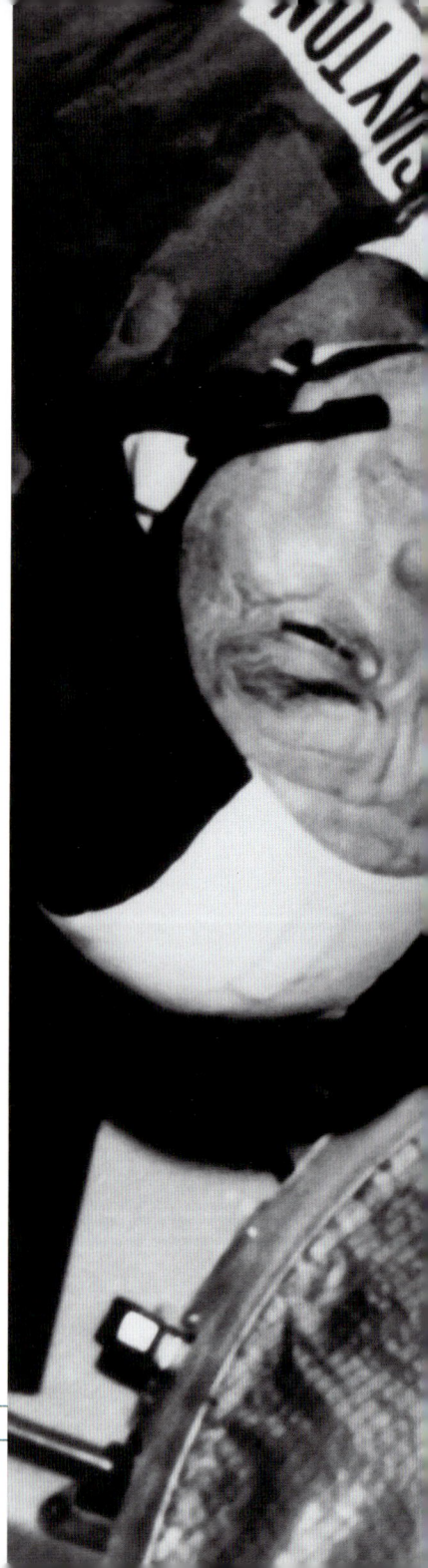

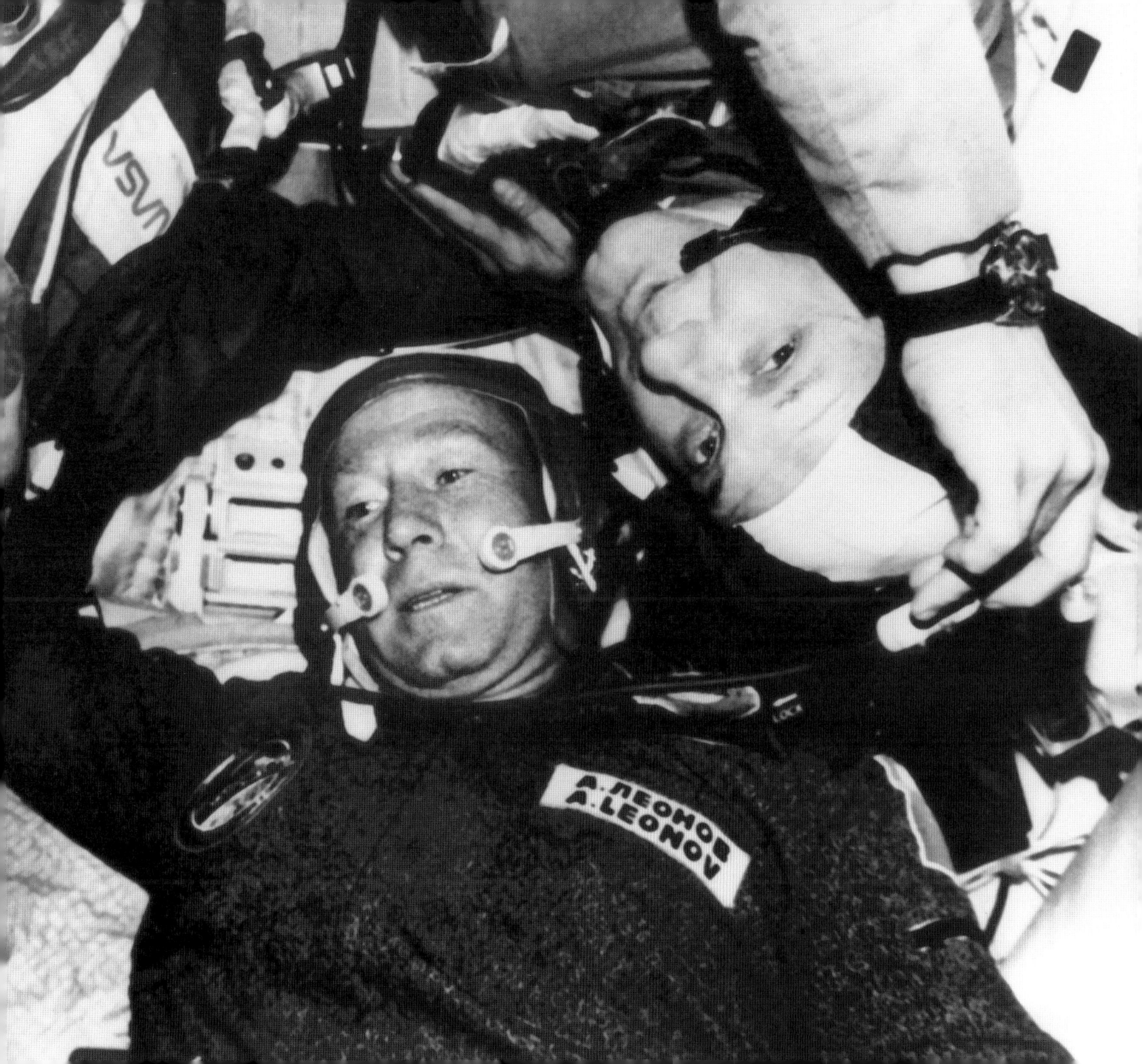

docking systems, and also revealed that, should a rescue in space be required, the two programs could undertake it together.

In a move that would eventually impact people worldwide, the Department of Defense launched a Navigation System Using Time and Ranging (NAVSTAR) satellite in 1978. It was the first satellite in a system that would later become commonly known as the global positioning system (GPS). By precisely knowing each satellite's position and the timing of its signals, GPS can pinpoint the location of a receiving device anywhere on Earth. It was first used by the military, but today it is used by ordinary people for everyday tasks such as getting driving directions. The last of the 24 satellites for the full initial NAVSTAR system was launched in 1994.

TI-99/4

Today Texas Instruments is known for high-end engineering calculators, but in 1979 the company released a home computer. The TI-99/4 was expensive compared to its competitors. It cost $1,150 because it came with a monitor, which was a modified Zenith television.[1] Sales were low both because of the price tag and because people realized you could hook the computer up to any television. Texas Instruments updated its computer and rereleased it in 1981, and although the company eventually sold 2.5 million computers, it decided it could not compete effectively and dropped this line of products.[2]

CONSUMER TECHNOLOGY

Consumer technology took off in the 1970s and included early versions of many products still used today. One of these items was the microwave oven. It had originally been invented in the mid-1940s, but the first models were massive and expensive.

Microwave ovens made cooking faster and easier.

HENRY EDWARD ROBERTS

Henry Edward Roberts served in the US Air Force before earning an electrical engineering degree at Oklahoma State University in 1968. In 1970, he founded Micro Instrumentation and Telemetry Systems (MITS) to sell electronic kits to hobbyists who built model rockets. He then developed a calculator parts kit that was featured on the cover of *Popular Electronics* magazine in November 1971, making plenty of money in sales from those kits in 1973. Like other popular electronics, calculators were very expensive to purchase until numerous manufacturers entered the market and forced the price down. Roberts searched for a new electronic product to sell.

Using the Intel 8080 microprocessor, which Roberts arranged to buy at a volume discount, he proceeded to create a kit for the Altair 8800 computer. Like the calculator, only a knowledgeable person with a soldering iron could assemble it. The computer was featured on the cover of *Popular Electronics* in January 1975. Electronics hobbyists submitted orders, eager to build their own minicomputers. In 1977, as prices dropped, Roberts sold his company and got out of the technology business, becoming a vegetable farmer. He later went back to college and earned a medical degree in 1986.

Henry Edward Roberts was known for his interest in invention and discovering new things.

By 1975, they were small enough to keep on the kitchen counter and were affordable, but only 4 percent of US homes had one. By 1976, this number jumped to 14 percent.[3]

Telephone technology was changing too. In 1973, the first call was made from a mobile phone manufactured by Motorola. The brick-shaped phone weighed approximately 2.4 pounds (1.1 kg) and had to be charged for ten hours before it could be used for 30 minutes. The phone that Motorola executive Martin Cooper used was a prototype to show what was possible, but the phone would not be available for people to buy for another ten years. It had push buttons, not a touch screen, to use when dialing.

The first home computers were introduced in the 1970s. In January 1975, Micro Instrumentation and Telemetry Systems (MITS), a small company owned by Henry Edward Roberts, released the Altair 8800. Described as a minicomputer, it was sold unassembled, though buyers could pay extra for an assembled version. The computer had no monitor or keyboard but instead included a series of switches for input and lights for output. Additional hardware had to be

ALTAIR ASSEMBLY

Putting a minicomputer together wasn't just a matter of snapping parts together. The Altair arrived with the circuit board and all of the resistors, diodes, lights, and other electronics needed to build the computer, but each component had to be soldered into place. In the process of soldering, a metal known as solder is melted and used to bridge the gap between two electronic components. Once it cools, it will conduct electricity. Users needed to heat a soldering iron, touch it and a strand of solder to the desired joint, neatly melt the solder, and then wipe off the soldering iron, all without getting burned. People without electrical experience had a hard time putting the computer together and finding and repairing any cold joints, which are bad solder points that do not conduct electricity.

purchased to connect the Altair to a monitor. The computer was hard for an inexperienced hobbyist to assemble, but within three months MITS had 4,000 orders waiting to be filled.[4] Realizing that these new computers would need software, on April 4, 1975, Bill Gates and Paul Allen founded Microsoft. Microsoft wrote programs for the Altair.

As is often the case, similar new products were being simultaneously developed. Steve Wozniak and Steve Jobs developed and produced the Apple I, a computer that went on sale in July 1976. The personal computers were hand-built by Wozniak, but buyers had to supply a case, keyboard, and monitor.

In the 1970s, these were not home computers for word processing or game play. Instead, the minicomputers were marketed to hobbyists, people interesting in electronics and building their own equipment. It wasn't until the 1980s that the costs of premade computers dropped enough to make them marketable to home users.

THREE MILE ISLAND

Because nuclear power was considered a safe source of electricity, the United States developed a nuclear energy program. One US nuclear power plant, Three Mile Island, was located outside of Middletown, Pennsylvania.

The Apple II computer came out in 1977, soon after the Apple I.

The first Three Mile Island reactor was completed and began operation in 1974, and the second came online in 1978.

On March 28, 1979, a failure occurred in a nonnuclear section of the second reactor. Water quit flowing into the cooling system that removed heat from the reactor's core. The reactor automatically shut down, but a coolant valve that vented water into the atmosphere stuck open. Human errors and instrument malfunctions eventually led to the core becoming exposed, and some radioactive gases got into the atmosphere. The governor advised pregnant women and children under the age of five years to evacuate nearby areas, leading to a panicked mass evacuation even while others sheltered in their homes.

No one was ultimately harmed, but the incident shook the public's faith in nuclear power. Studies revealed the radiation the public was exposed to was less than they would have received from a chest X-ray, but scientists and the public still questioned what it might do to people, plants, and animals in the area. Seven other reactors similar to those at Three Mile Island were shut down temporarily. No utility companies ordered the construction of new reactors until the mid-1980s.

The Three Mile Island incident caused the government to tighten the safety protocols of nuclear plant operations.

Singer Stevie Wonder burst onto the music scene in the 1960s, but he received critical success in the 1970s with albums such as *Talking Book*, *Innervisions*, *Music of My Mind*, and *Songs in the Key of Life*.

CHAPTER SIX

POP CULTURE OF
THE 1970s

The music of the 1970s featured a great variety in sound, in part made possible because of the eight-track recorders that became available in the late 1960s. This meant that lead vocals could be recorded on one track, with separate tracks for additional vocals, guitars, drums, synthesizers, and special effects. Bands could experiment with how they combined these tracks into a master recording, creating a diverse mix of sounds. The recordings themselves were more affordable than before, since a new process made creating vinyl records less expensive. All a music lover needed was a record player to listen to the latest sounds.

As artists experimented, hard rock got harder, louder, and more rebellious with bands such as KISS, Led Zeppelin, Alice Cooper, and Black Sabbath

creating different sounds. Hard rock bands, especially KISS, became known for the onstage spectacles they created in concert as much as for their music. KISS's look included black and white stage makeup and black clothing with spikes. The band made use of lights and pyrotechnic effects reflecting off smoke, all in front of huge speaker banks.

Simultaneously, soft rock became softer, with radio stations specializing in the genre known as easy listening. Popular musicians included ABBA, the Carpenters, and Barry Manilow. Many young music lovers made fun of this music, perhaps because their parents listened to it.

New varieties of music were developed in the 1970s, including punk, which protested against the uniformity of society. This music, played by bands such as

REST IN PEACE

The 1970s may have been a great time for music, but there were tragedies, especially when noteworthy musicians died of drug overdoses. Guitarist Jimi Hendrix passed away at age 27 on September 18, 1970, in London, England. He died of an overdose of barbiturates. Singer Janis Joplin was also only 27 years old when she died of a heroin overdose on October 4, 1970, in Los Angeles. Jim Morrison, lead singer for the psychedelic band the Doors, died of heart failure on July 3, 1971, at the age of 27 in his apartment in Paris, France. Drug use was suspected as the cause. In each case, fans mourned and continued to listen to their music.

KISS members had unique looks and put on wild shows for fans.

the Ramones, the Clash, and the Sex Pistols, was loud and confrontational. The New Wave genre also included cultural commentary, but the music was smoother and more polished. New Wave bands included the Pretenders, the Cars, and the Talking Heads.

Funk, associated with the Black pride movement, combined aspects of rock, rhythm and blues, and soul to generate a form of urban music driven by rhythm and danceability. James Brown, Parliament-Funkadelic, and Wild Cherry performed funk. This popular music ultimately influenced another type of dance music: disco. Disco featured a driving rhythm created by bass guitars and drum lines. People flocked to discotheques, the dance clubs that gave this music its name. Dancers executed showy moves in the shimmering light of mirrored balls suspended from ceilings. Disco was initially ignored by DJs and mainstream stations but caught on as people heard it in clubs. On the crowded dance floors of discotheques, or discos, men could dance with other men, groups of friends could dance together, and mixed-race

VCR

The original video cassette recorder (VCR), the VRX-1000, was invented in 1956 by the Ampex Corporation. The recorder was difficult to operate and cost tens of thousands of dollars. This put it out of reach of ordinary consumers, but television networks saw the advantages and invested in these machines, which enabled them to record and replay live broadcasts. Decades later, another company, JVC, invented a new VCR system called Video Home System (VHS). JVC introduced it in Japan in 1976 and then in the United States a year later. This 1977 VCR cost $1,280. The tapes cost $20 and could hold two hours of recording, making them a popular choice for some consumers.[1] The VCR allowed people to make recordings in their own homes and changed how they watched television.

Disco was the leading style of dance music in the 1970s.

couples could easily meet. Both patrons and artists included people from every social group. Popular artists in this genre included Gloria Gaynor, Van McCoy, and Barry White.

In New York's South Bronx neighborhood, young people took influences from funk, disco, and soul and created hip-hop. Jamaican DJ Clive Campbell, also known as Kool Herc, was the first to emphasize breaks in hip-hop music that indicated a musical change within a song. Hip-hop artists from this time include Grandmaster Flash, the Last Poets, and the Rock Steady Crew.

SMALL AND LARGE SCREENS

On Saturday mornings in the 1970s, many children spent time watching a variety of animated cartoons. Some, including *The Osmond Brothers* (1972), *The Jackson 5ive* (1971), and *Partridge Family 2200 A.D.* (1974), featured celebrity musical families. *Josie and the Pussycats* (1970) featured a fictitious band created for the cartoon. Other cartoons featured superheroes, including *Shazam* (1974) and *Spider-Woman* (1979).

On large movie screens, films were often dark and gritty. These included Francis Ford Coppola's *The Godfather* (1972),

SCHOOLHOUSE ROCK!

The original *Schoolhouse Rock!* television series premiered in 1973 and ran through 1979. The short animations could be seen on Saturday mornings between other cartoons. Each featured a catchy song for viewers to sing along to while they learned about topics such as the solar system, the Constitution, conjunctions, how a bill becomes a law, and much more. The interpretations were sometimes deeply flawed because they ignored potentially controversial topics like slavery and racism, but they introduced many US children to basic educational topics.

John Boorman's *Deliverance* (1972), and Martin Scorsese's *Taxi Driver* (1976). Other popular movies included summer blockbusters, films that were expensive to produce but were expected to generate a lot of income. Perhaps the first such movie was *Jaws*, which was released in 1975, directed by Steven Spielberg. This was the first US movie to earn more than $235 million, and it set the standard for blockbusters that followed.[2]

Another blockbuster was in production for four years because of the special effects involved. *Star Wars* (1977) was directed by George Lucas and earned $3 million its first week, even though it opened in only 42 theaters nationwide.[3] The special effects alone revolutionized the film industry.

In 1975, home gaming joined television and movies as a form of on-screen entertainment. That year, Atari introduced a home version of its popular arcade ping-pong game, *Pong*. A gamer could play against a friend by turning one of two dials on the console to move the paddle up and down

VIDEO ARCADES

The first arcade games were pinball machines that came out in the 1930s. The earliest racing game with a steering wheel, *Grand Prix*, came out in 1969 and made developers think about what other types of controls and gaming scenarios they could come up with. In the 1970s, more games were introduced. *Space Invaders* was released in 1978 by Taito, followed by Namco's *Galaxian* in 1979. With popular, kid-friendly games, food chains such as Chuck E. Cheese installed games in their restaurants. Arcade games were coin operated. Players would come in with a handful of quarters, eager to see how much game time they could buy with each coin.

the screen to hit the ball. The home console hooked up to a television, but with no cartridges, it played only this one game. In spite of this limitation, it was the year's most in-demand toy. By 1977, Atari had developed the Atari Video Computer System (VCS). There were nine game cartridges available, including *Air-Sea Battle*, *Star Ship*, *Blackjack*, *Street Racer*, and *Indy 500*.

TOP TOYS

In 1970, Nerf released its first soft foam ball designed for indoor play, because, as it said in the ad, "You can't damage lamps or break windows."[4] The ad helped sell millions of foam balls in 1970, and Nerf quickly developed the Nerf Flying Disk, also marketed as an indoor toy.

Although the skateboard was introduced in the 1960s, it became more popular in the 1970s with two inventions. In 1972, Frank Nasworthy created the Cadillac wheel, a urethane wheel that gave boards a smoother ride. However, the wheel bearings were still exposed, so sand and grit could work their way in and compromise the ride. This was solved in the mid-1970s when the Road Rider wheel with sealed bearings became available. With smooth-riding wheels and enclosed bearings, demand for skateboards took off.

Developments in electronics led to new types of toys. This technology made the first handheld electronic games possible, and Mattel introduced *Electronic Football* in 1977. The game's graphics were basic, with red rectangle players moving across a black field. Despite this, it was one of 1977's most requested toys. The toy that equaled *Electronic Football* in popularity was another electronic game, Milton Bradley's *Simon*. The game featured four buttons, each a different color. The game

Improvements to skateboards made it possible for skaters to do new tricks.

would flash a pattern, such as red, red, blue, yellow, green, and the player had to press the buttons in sequence to repeat it. In 1978, the most popular toy was Speak & Spell by Texas Instruments. It would say a word, and the user would then key in the correct spelling. It wasn't the first talking toy, but it was both durable and reliable. With these successes, electronic toys were here to stay.

One popular pattern in the 1970s was paisley. This is a colorful design made with curved shapes.

In February 1970, some new fashions by Black designers were showcased in New York City.

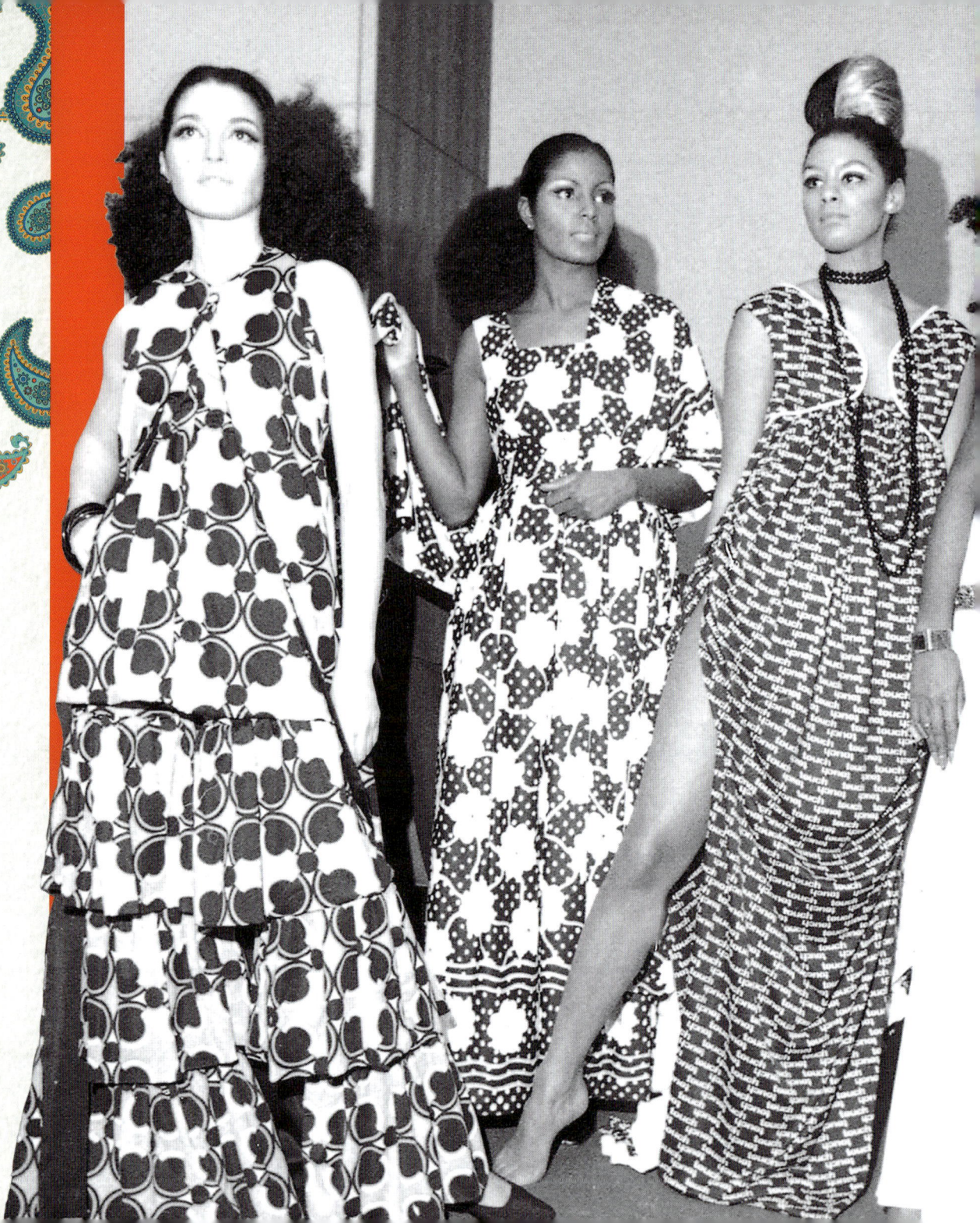

CHAPTER SEVEN

FASHION OF THE 1970s

The availability of synthetic fabrics changed how people dressed in the 1970s. These artificial fibers were often cheaper than natural fibers, especially silk or linen. With these fabrics, many fashionable and ready-to-wear clothes were less expensive than tailored, custom-fitted clothing. This meant that more people could afford fashionable clothing.

Synthetic fabric was so common that the 1970s was known as the polyester decade among designers. The double-knit polyester fabrics didn't breathe, so the garments tended to be hot to wear. However, the fabric was versatile and gave rise to men's suits in a wide variety of colors and patterns. Jackets often had wide, notched lapels, and suits often came with vests. Men shopped from lines of mixable suits, purchasing two jackets, a vest, several

pairs of trousers, dress shirts, and ties that could be combined to create a variety of looks for a complete workweek. In addition, disco influenced fashion as men bought silk dress shirts. Women might wear silk blouses and wide-legged pants or miniskirts.

CASUAL DRESSING

The earliest 1970s fashions took their inspiration from the 1960s. Like the 1960s, the 1970s placed an emphasis on handmade designs, incorporating things like tie-dye into fashion. In the 1960s, this had been about rejecting mainstream, consumer fashion. In the 1970s, designers and clothing companies seized on the popularity of these handcrafted looks and made the appearance, if not the process, of actually handcrafting these items, part of high fashion. Handmade clothing included patchwork vests, crocheted tops, and embroidery.

Prairie dresses were another popular style. From midlength to maxi, the dresses featured tiered skirts, floral prints, and lace panels. Some were

DIANE VON FURSTENBERG

Diane von Furstenberg was a Belgian-American designer. She created a dress style that is still worn today. In an attempt to make a dress that could be worn by every body type, von Furstenberg wanted a relaxed dress made with casual fabric. She chose jersey, a type of knit fabric. First, she created a skirt that she paired with a wrap top. Only later did she create the wrap-style dress. She originally made it in silk, but later the style came to be made in a variety of stretchy, easy-to-care-for fabrics in bright colors and prints. It was versatile and could be worn casually or for a dressy event. It revolutionized women's fashion. But for Furstenberg, her work is about more than the designs. "This brand is about the relationship I have with women," she said.[1]

Tie-dye allowed people to wear colorful and unique designs.

Farrah Fawcett, *top,* with her Charlie's Angels costars Kate Jackson, *left,* and Jaclyn Smith, *right*

sleeveless, while others featured long sleeves gathered around the wrist. Popular designers included Gunne Sax and Bill Gibb.

Casual clothing in the 1970s included denim, with children and teens wearing denim jeans. Men wore jeans and denim suits. Women's denim clothing was more diverse and included skirts, dresses, jumpsuits, jackets, and more.

Another casual look in the late 1970s was sportswear. This look wasn't just for people doing workouts. The style included sweatshirts, casual skirts, leotards, and leggings for women. Polo shirts, athletic shorts, and T-shirts of every kind were worn by men, women, and children.

CLASSIC STYLES

Not all clothing in the 1970s was casual or sporty. Designers also looked to the past for classic styles for work and evening wear. Men's formal suits were based on the golden era of Hollywood in the 1920s and 1930s, with loosely draped vests, jackets, and trousers.

FARRAH FAWCETT

Actress and model Farrah Fawcett embodied the fashions popular with teens and adult women. Her look included casual sportswear, suitable for fighting crime in her role on *Charlie's Angels* or playing in a tennis match, and glamorous, flowing gowns for public appearances. Dressed up or dressed down, her style was simple. This style is reflected in the best-selling poster of all time, which shows Fawcett wearing a red one-piece swimsuit and smiling at the camera. An original copy of the 1976 poster is part of the collection at the Smithsonian National Museum of American History. Often, it was Fawcett's feathered hair that others tried to copy. The layered haircut can be worn straight or curled, but it frames the person's face and tends to look big. It often has a lot of texture. This was a haircut that both men and women copied in the 1970s.

In 1971, French fashion designer Yves Saint Laurent created a line of women's wear inspired by the 1940s. This collection, known as Liberation, featured turbans, boxy fur jackets, and crepe dresses. Wide-legged trousers were paired with silky, sleeveless blouses or jackets that looked like men's suit coats. Tulip-cut, knee-length skirts were combined with scoop-necked blouses. The line was considered scandalous because certain garments resembled clothing worn by prostitutes during World War II. But Saint Laurent shrugged off the criticism, saying that the young people he designed his clothing for wouldn't have these preconceptions.

Saint Laurent and other designers also created clothing for women that looked much like menswear. Fashion commentators believe that as women gained more rights and more sexual freedom, women's fashion changed as well. Fashion icon Bianca Jagger wore a white tuxedo by the designer Halston. Pantsuits or trouser suits came in every imaginable color or combination as women dressed for the workplace.

JACKIE KENNEDY

During the 1960s, when her husband John F. Kennedy was president, Jackie Kennedy wore classic suits, and women copied her look. In the 1970s, Kennedy went for a whole new look, adopting patterned maxi dresses and wrap dresses. When traveling or outdoors, she was often photographed wearing oversized sunglasses. Women across the country continued to copy her look.

CHILDREN AND TEENS

In many ways clothing for teens in the 1970s mirrored clothing for adults. Teen boys wore wide-collared suits in both solid fabrics and plaids. Both boys and girls wore denim, including bell-bottom jeans and miniskirts for teen girls.

Teen fashions often mirrored the clothing young people saw on their music idols. Some teen girls donned the free-flowing kaftans worn by Joni Mitchell. Others wore the denim and leather of punk musicians. The distinctive punk look included ripped fishnet stockings with short black dresses, torn jeans with band T-shirts, studded jewelry, safety pins, and Dr. Martens boots.

Teen girls in particular also wore a variety of looks inspired by clothing from around the world. These included Mexican peasant blouses and flare-legged gaucho pants that hit just below the knee. Bold patterns reminiscent of those seen on clothing in Africa and India were also popular.

But there were also clothing trends seen only among younger children, including flame-resistant sleepwear. Footie pajamas, two-piece sets, and quilted robes all came complete with the addition of a chemical flame retardant. The sales pitch was that if there were a house fire, children would be more likely to escape safely if their pajamas couldn't catch on fire. Then the Consumer Product Safety Commission discovered that the chemical flame retardants could

DIANA ROSS

Whether she was on stage singing with the Supremes or appearing in the pages of a magazine, Diana Ross inspired women in the 1970s with her sense of glamour. Whenever Ross appeared in white linen, a glittery jumpsuit, or a sequined gown, she was always accessorized. Ross was famous for her false eyelashes, dramatic eye shadow, dazzling earrings, and hats and other hair accessories. Ross wore everything with flair and fashion, showing off the variety of trends available to women in the 1970s.

possibly lead to cancer. Congress banned the manufacture of these chemicals in 1979 under the Toxic Substances Control Act.

While teens were copying their punk idols, younger children were dressed in clothes featuring *Sesame Street* characters. This Public Broadcasting Service (PBS) television show debuted in 1969 and grew in popularity throughout the 1970s. Pictures of Bert and Ernie, Oscar the Grouch, and more were on crocheted sweaters, raincoats, pajamas, and more.

Another children's clothing trend was matching outfits. Whether it was for a family party or a portrait photo, children were dressed in matching outfits that ranged from prairie skirts and white blouses to denim suits with white turtlenecks. The problem of finding matching outfits for boys and girls was solved with the handmade granny-square vest with patterns available that could be adapted for young children or teen boys.

Denim and bell-bottoms were a popular fashion choice in the 1970s.

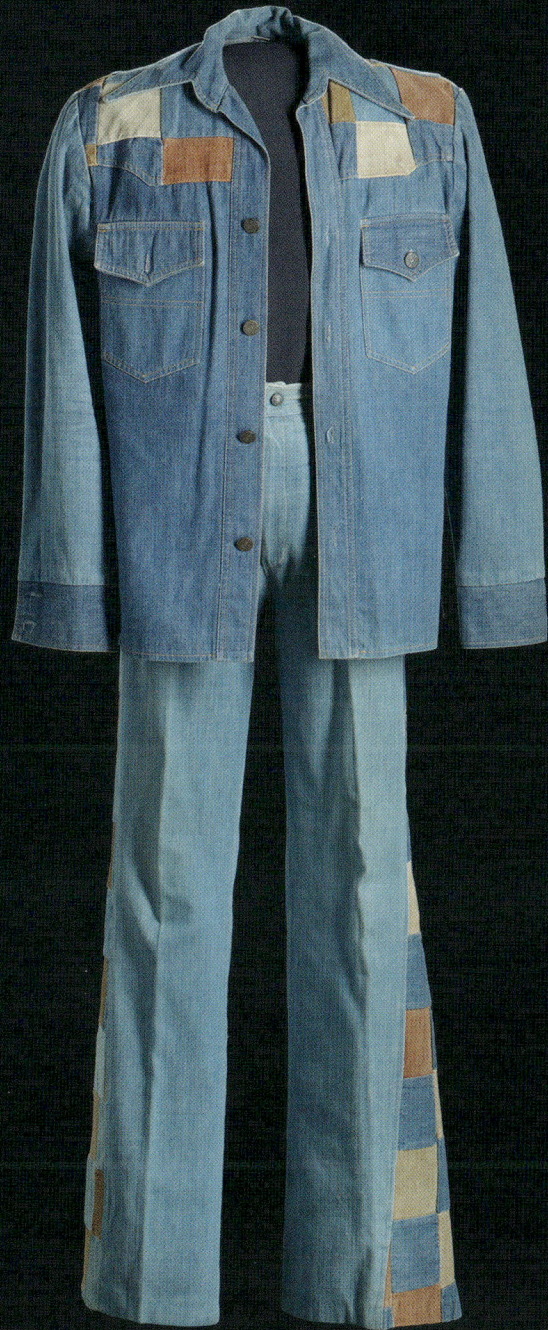

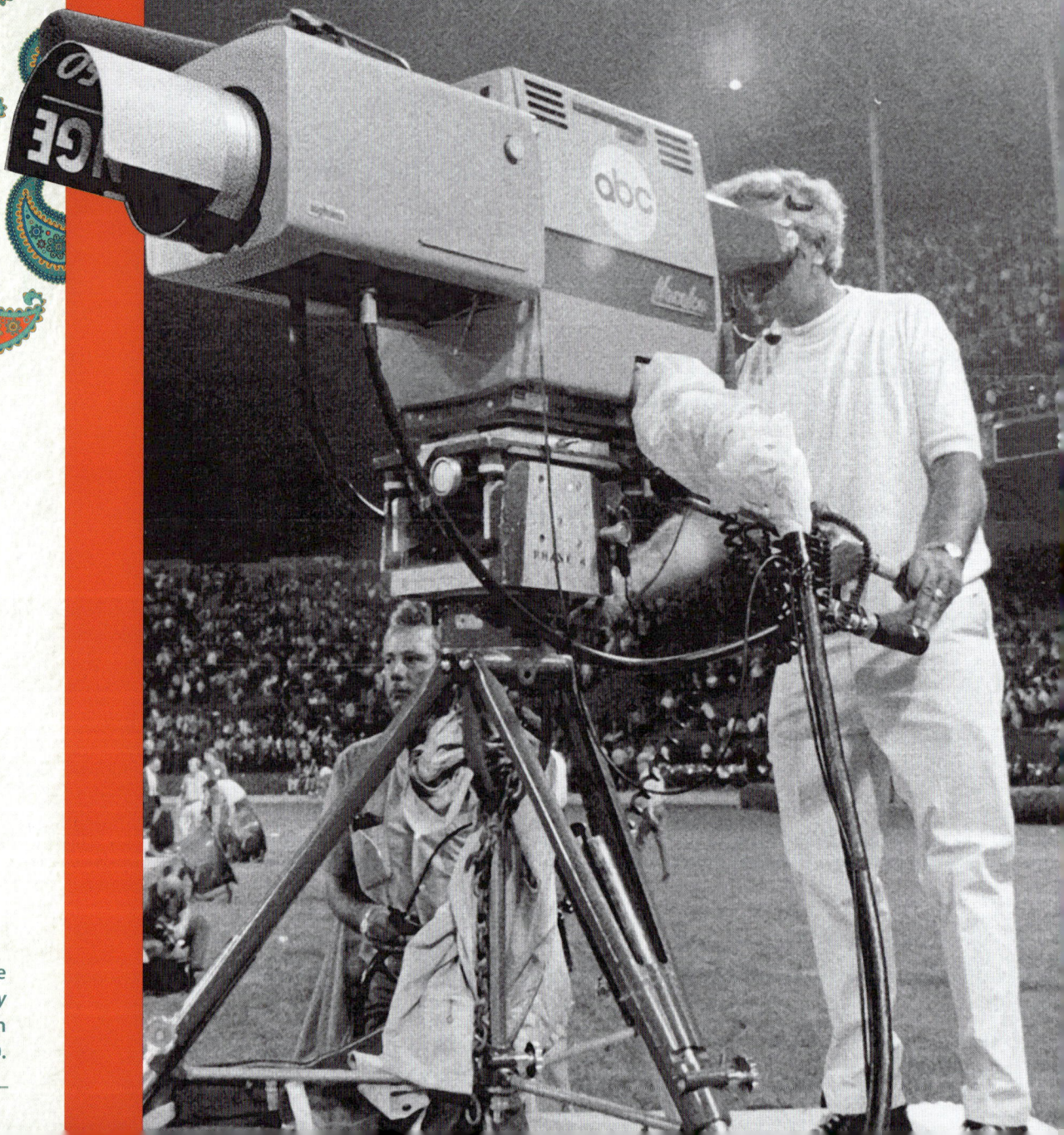

A cameraman stands on the sidelines during a *Monday Night Football* game in September 1970.

CHAPTER EIGHT

SPORTS
OF THE 1970s

Money brought big changes to professional sports in the 1970s. National Football League (NFL) commissioner Pete Rozelle reached a deal with the ABC television network to air *Monday Night Football*. The network agreed to pay the NFL $25.5 million for three years starting in 1970.[1] Before the first year was out, *Monday Night Football* had become one of the most popular sports programs on television. Major League Baseball (MLB) and other sports leagues received similar lucrative broadcast deals.

With so much money changing hands, players' unions demanded that the athletes themselves get a share, and the amount of money earned by players started to rise. In 1972, Bobby Hull of the National Hockey League (NHL) signed

a ten-year deal for $1 million with the Winnipeg Jets.[2] Some people thought this was a ridiculous amount of money to pay an athlete, but it was only the beginning. In 1978, baseball's Dave Parker signed with the Pittsburgh Pirates for five years for $5 million.[3] This made Parker the first athlete to earn $1 million in a single year.

The development of free agency in 1975 made contracts like Parker's possible. Marvin Miller, the head of the MLB Players Association, was a former United Steelworkers Union official with experience negotiating contracts. He helped negotiate a ruling by an arbitration panel that said an athlete who had played on a team for six years but whose current contract had been unsigned by the team for a year could become a free agent. This would allow a small number of

Marvin Miller, *center*, fought for fair compensation for MLB players.

> ### TRIPLE CROWN
> Only three-year-old horses can enter three prestigious races in thoroughbred horse racing. The Kentucky Derby is run at Churchill Downs in Louisville, Kentucky, most often on the first Saturday in May. The Preakness Stakes is run on the third Saturday in May at the Pimlico Race Course in Baltimore, Maryland. The Belmont Stakes is in June, and it takes place at Belmont Park in Elmont, New York. A Triple Crown winner is a horse that wins all three of those races. Between 1875 and 2022, this had only happened 13 times, including three times in the 1970s. In 1973, Secretariat was the first horse to win the Triple Crown in 25 years. Seattle Slew won in 1977, followed by Affirmed in 1978.

RUNNING

In the 1970s, running became popular as a form of recreation. The Seattle Marathon was first run in 1970. New York City began holding a marathon in 1972, the same year that Frank Shorter won a gold medal in the marathon for Team USA in the Munich Olympics. Shorter inspired Americans to take up running, and it turned into a way for Americans to get fit. A form of recreational running known as jogging emerged. It gave rise to an industry that included athletic shoes, clothing, and how-to tapes and books.

players each year to switch teams. Talented athletes could negotiate higher salaries as teams bid against each other to gain the best players.

MLB

Baseball was popular through the 1970s. Two teams dominated this decade: the Baltimore Orioles and the Cincinnati Reds. In 1970 and 1971, the Orioles were led by Frank Robinson. He helped the team win four pennants (1966, 1969, 1970, and 1971) and the World Series in 1966 and 1970. Robinson also became only the eleventh player in major league history to hit 500 career home runs. He left the Orioles in 1975 and went to the Cleveland Indians—now known as the Cleveland Guardians—where he became the league's first Black manager.

Led by Pete Rose, the Cincinnati Reds were the most successful National League team from 1970 to 1976. In 1970, Rose signed a contract for six figures. This was the same year he led the National League team to a win in the All-Star Game. In 1972, Rose played as a left-fielder and led the league in hits (198) and at-bats (645). In 1973, Rose won his third and final batting title, a recognition of the player with the best batting average. His average was .338 that year.

A big change came to baseball in 1973 when the American League began to use designated hitters. This allowed another player to bat in place of a pitcher. Pitchers are often poor hitters, so having a designated hitter can improve a team's offensive play.

On April 8, 1974, while playing for the Atlanta Braves, Hank Aaron hit his 715th career home run. With this homer he broke the record set by Babe Ruth. Ruth's record of 714 home runs had been set in 1935. Aaron retired in 1976 with a career total of 755 home runs.

WOMEN IN SPORTS

The 1970s was also a great time for women in sports. On June 23, 1972, Title IX of the Education Amendments became law. It states that "no person in the United States shall, on the basis of sex, be excluded from participation in, be denied the benefits of, or be subjected to discrimination under any education program or activity receiving federal financial assistance."[4] In 1975, provisions that forbade sex discrimination in athletic programs were signed into law, and schools were given three years to comply. This meant that schools started funding women's teams and athletic programs. Women now had the opportunity to train and compete in high school and college athletics.

Several powerful tennis players including Chris Evert and Billie Jean King drew crowds throughout the 1970s. In 1973, King was challenged by aging male tennis player Bobby Riggs, known for his chauvinism and controversial statements, to a match called the Battle of the Sexes. Riggs had been ranked number one in the world of tennis in the 1940s, and earlier in the year he had already challenged and soundly defeated top women's tennis player Margaret Court. Riggs had

BILLIE JEAN
KING

Billie Jean King's tennis career took off in her teens. She and Karen Hantz won the Wimbledon doubles championship in 1961. By her 1984 retirement, King had won a record 20 Wimbledon titles.

Although female tennis players worked just as hard as men, they continually had fewer opportunities to compete for prizes and prestige. In protest of this discrepancy, King and eight other players, known as the Original 9, organized the Virginia Slims Circuit. The US Lawn Tennis Association threatened to suspend anyone who signed up to compete, but the Original 9 signed on to play for the symbolic amount of $1 each.[5] This circuit later became the Women's Tennis Association (WTA) in 1973, with King as its president. The group remains the primary organizing body for women's tennis. It governs the WTA Tour, the worldwide women's tennis tour. With her 1973 victory over Bobby Riggs, King received the prize money and used the win as a launching point to speak out for women's sports and female players. She continued to do that into the 2020s.

Throughout her career, Billie Jean King won 39 major titles.

challenged King before, but this time she couldn't ignore him. She had to show the world that a woman could win.

On September 20, 1973, King and Riggs arrived at the Houston Astrodome, ready to compete. An estimated 90 million people around the world tuned in to watch this televised event. King defeated Riggs in three sets and won the cash prize of $100,000.[6] King later admitted that she had felt pressured to win, not because she was worried that she wouldn't, but because a loss would discourage and demoralize women. "To beat a 55-year-old guy was no thrill for me. The thrill was exposing a lot of new people to tennis," said King.[7]

OLYMPIC GAMES

In 1972, the Summer Olympic Games were held in Munich, Germany. It was an eventful time for Team USA, with Mark Spitz dominating swimming. Not only did he win seven gold medals, but he set seven records in the 100-meter men's freestyle, the 200-meter men's freestyle, the

TERRORISM AT THE OLYMPICS

On September 5, 1972, Palestinian militants belonging to the group Black September climbed a fence surrounding the Olympic Village in Munich where athletes lived during the Games. Dressed as athletes and using stolen keys, they forced their way into the quarters of the Israeli Olympic team. One coach was killed, and ten athletes, coaches, and officials were taken hostage. The militants demanded to be taken by helicopter to Fürstenfeldbruck Air Base where the gunmen believed they would be given a plane for escape, but a rescue operation had been planned. Unfortunately, it was poorly coordinated. In the end, 20 hours after it all started, 11 Israelis, one Munich policeman, and five terrorists had been killed, with three other terrorists captured.[8]

100-meter men's butterfly, the 200-meter men's butterfly, and three relay events. Spitz held the record for most gold medals won at a single Olympic Games by an American athlete until it was broken by swimmer Michael Phelps, who won eight gold medals in 2008.

It was also at the 1972 Summer Games that the United States played against the Soviet Union in men's basketball. As the game neared its end, the United States was in the lead 50–49, but then a timeout was called. After the Soviets inbounded the ball, the horn sounded an American win. The US team was shocked when they were told to stop cheering and resume play. A mistake had been made, and the Soviet team was given another chance to score. It did, and the Soviets won the game. The US team refused to claim its silver medals.

At the 1976 Summer Games in Montreal, Canada, Caitlyn Jenner, who was known at the time as Bruce Jenner, was the men's decathlon champion for Team USA. Jenner won the gold and also set a world record. The decathlon thoroughly tests an athlete's abilities and range with ten separate

CAITLYN JENNER

In 2015, Caitlyn Jenner became the most well-known athlete to come out as transgender with a cover photo on *Vanity Fair* magazine. Transitioning in the public eye brought Caitlyn Jenner both praise and criticism, but she continued to be a champion for transgender rights. Jenner made an attempt at a political career, running as a Republican for California governor in the 2021 recall election of Gavin Newsom. Jenner ultimately lost, but she remained an inspiration for many people in the transgender community.

track-and-field events, including the long jump, high jump, shot put, pole vault, javelin, discus, 110-meter hurdles, 100-meter race, 400-meter race, and 1,500-meter race. A photo of Jenner's victory lap carrying an American flag captures an iconic moment in Olympic history. Back in the United States, Jenner was featured on Wheaties cereal boxes and became a motivational speaker.

Historical markers around Kent State remind people of what happened on May 4, 1970.

MAY 4, 19
JEFFREY MILL

CHAPTER NINE

THE LEGACY OF THE 1970s

The Kent State massacre at the start of the 1970s shapes the awareness and attitudes of the students that attend the school today. They are reminded of the events of that day whenever they walk past a commemorative marker for a wounded student or the bullet hole in Solar Totem #1, a sculpture by Don Drumm that was struck by a stray bullet. For some people, it is a reminder that students can die standing up for what they believe in. For school administrators, it can be an important reminder that student voices matter.

In the 1970s, people protested about more rights for women and a lower voting age. The extension of voting rights to people as young as 18 continues to affect elections. Elizabeth Matto is an associate research professor at the

Eagleton Institute of Politics at Rutgers University. She talked to PBS about Generation Z and the impact of these young people on politics today. Generation Z often refers to people who were born between 1997 and 2012. "It is a generation that cares about public problems, wants to solve public problems, and most importantly, sees politics or the use of political institutions as a way to solve those problems," said Matto.[1]

Matto also thinks Generation Z is going to use political institutions and politicians in unexpected ways. This is because Generation Z is diverse, politically active, and often not tied to political labels. That means Generation Z may not simply vote along party lines. Instead, they may support candidates who are concerned about the same things that they are, such as the environment, economic opportunities, and access to health care. What they care about will become increasingly important as more and more members of Generation Z reach voting age.

DEALING WITH THE MASSACRE

After the Kent State massacre, the administration built a gym on the parking lot where students had been shot. It even tried to rebrand the school, encouraging people to call it simply Kent instead of Kent State. In 1990, Carol Cartwright became the university's president and sent out an internal questionnaire about the school's mission. She didn't ask about the shootings, but many answers focused on the massacre as people asked the administration to not erase what had happened. Memorials and a museum were installed on campus to remember the massacre.

TITLE IX

Another legacy of the 1970s has been in women's sports. A large part of this is due to Title IX. Donna de Varona was a swimmer who medaled in the Olympics. She's also a sports journalist, and she chaired the organizing committee for the 1999 FIFA Women's World Cup. In 1964, de Varona won two gold medals in the Tokyo Summer Olympics, one in the 400-meter individual medley and the other in the 4x100 freestyle relay, but then she quit competing. De Varona explained why to the International Olympic Committee. "People often ask me why I stopped swimming competitively at the age of 17. I'd beaten 18 world records, won 37 national titles and achieved two Olympic gold medals. . . . There was no Title IX in the federal law in my day. High-level women's university sport . . . was not there to help female athletes extend a career at the peak of their physical performance and prowess," said de Varona. At the time, very few women competed in university sports. "In the early 1970s, around 50,000 men went to university thanks to sports scholarships, compared to around 50 women, and at high school, only one girl in 27 practiced any kind of sports activity," said de Varona.[2] With Title IX, women can earn sports scholarships and participate in college sports organized by the National Collegiate Athletic Association (NCAA).

MAKING CUTS

People sometimes blame Title IX when a school drops a men's sport. The belief that women's sports exist at the expense of men's sports is one of the most persistent myths about Title IX. In 2018, *Forbes* magazine looked at various studies that examined athletic programs, money spent, and the number of participants. *Forbes* found that sports that get cut tend to generate very little income. The money from the cut sports does not then go into women's sports. Instead, it often goes into football or men's basketball—two sports that generate a lot of revenue when a school has a strong team. Sports make money through ticket sales, corporate sponsorships, alumni donations, and more.

Women still make only a small fraction of what male athletes earn. This was seen in 2019 when comparing the average pay for various sports. The average pay for a male National Basketball Association player was $8.3 million. For female players in the Women's National Basketball Association, it was $75,181. In golf, a male Professional Golfers Association athlete made on average $1.2 million compared to a Ladies Professional Golfers Association athlete at $48,993. In tennis, the difference was less extreme but still notable. A male Association of Tennis Professionals player made on average $335,946 compared to a Woman's Tennis Association player's $283,635.[3] The good news is that women have more opportunities to compete in elite tennis, basketball, soccer, and golf. Title IX helped make that happen, even though there is still progress to be made to gain true equality in sports.

STAR WARS

Many movies from the 1970s, including *Jaws*, are still popular. But no other film from the decade has had the lasting impact of *Star Wars*. The effect of *Star Wars* on popular culture is undeniable. Throughout the years, this series has sprouted sequels and prequels, animated films, novels, comic books, television shows, games, toys, T-shirts, and more. The original

The passing of Title IX in the 1970s has allowed girls today to play a variety of school sports.

trilogy has had a huge influence on how movies are made, creating a class of blockbusters filled with special effects, including *The Matrix* (1999) and *The Lord of the Rings: The Fellowship of the Ring* (2001).

Star Wars also revived space science fiction as a genre in cinema. In the 1930s, space science fiction had been popular, with comics such as *Buck Rogers* and *Flash Gordon* adapted as movies. *Star Trek* was an inexpensively made show produced in 1966, but it wasn't until after the success of *Star Wars* that a *Star Trek* movie was produced for the big screen.

Star Wars director George Lucas helped other filmmakers see that movie merchandise could make as much as the movies themselves. The action figures that Kenner Products made were wildly successful, and the demand was overwhelming. *Star Wars* toys also introduced the idea of toys as collectibles. From the 1970s on, people purchased *Star Wars* toys and kept

STAR WARS DAY

May 4 is known as *Star Wars* Day. Every year on this date, social media is flooded with *Star Wars*–related posts and memes. Many of them feature the phrase "May the 4th be with you," a play on the well-known *Star Wars* saying, "May the force be with you." The first large-scale celebration of *Star Wars* Day was organized in 2011 at the Underground Cinema in Toronto, Canada. The theater held a trivia competition, costume contest, and more.

The cast of *Star Wars*, including Carrie Fisher, *left*, Mark Hamill, *center*, and Harrison Ford, *right*, was well-known into the 2020s.

them for collectible purposes, often considering them an investment.

TECH AND COMPUTERS

By the end of the 1970s, electronic devices were becoming mainstream products. Personal computers remained rare, but their popularity was beginning to extend beyond only hobbyists. Over the following decades, computers steadily became more powerful and more useful. By the 2020s, using a computer of some kind was a necessity for participating in modern society. The desktops, laptops, tablets, and smartphones of today are the distant descendants of devices like the Altair 8800, which first brought computers into people's homes.

Whenever the impacts of this technology are discussed, some people focus on the negatives. They say that young people have too many screens distracting them. They mention the problems with online bullying and say that excessive screen time can contribute to obesity and depression. But there are also many positives. Teachers and schools use computers as classroom tools. Some teachers conduct lessons on smart boards. They may even

STAR WARS TOYS

Star Wars movies have earned more than $7 billion in box office sales, and the toys have earned twice that amount.[4] Before *Star Wars*, no movie had led to a toy line, so it isn't surprising that most toy companies George Lucas approached were not interested in *Star Wars* toys. Only Kenner Products was willing to sign a deal. But by the Christmas after the movie launched, only the simplest toys were made, including puzzles, board games, and paint sets. Then Kenner decided to take it a step further and made the *Star Wars* Early Bird Certificate Package. This was a box with stickers and a certificate that young fans could fill out and return to guarantee they would get an action figure set when it was ready in the spring of 1978. The action figures proved to be incredibly popular.

Today, *Star Wars* toys are found in stores around the world.

assign homework online. In 2020, a disease called COVID-19 spread around the world and killed many people. To help slow the disease's spread, many US states locked down. That impacted a lot of schools, which moved to online learning to keep their students from getting sick. Laptops, tablets, and internet service made it possible for teachers to stay connected with their students and teach them remotely. A familiarity with screens and technology may also encourage students to study technology and pursue technological careers.

The impact of the 1970s goes beyond sports, *Star Wars*, and computers. Many of the things that concerned young people in the 1970s were still important in the 2020s. Energy and the environment continued to be political talking points. So were increasing opportunities for marginalized people and working against political corruption. The 1970s was a decade of varied fashion and film that people were still able to enjoy decades later.

The 1970s inspired many looks that some people like to replicate today.

TIMELINE

1970

- The US Census expands its questions to gather information about people with Hispanic heritage.

- The first soft foam Nerf ball is released.

- In April, the Apollo 13 accident occurs.

- On April 22, people celebrate the first Earth Day.

- On April 30, President Richard Nixon announces the expansion of the Vietnam War into Cambodia.

- On May 4, four students are killed by National Guardsmen in the Kent State massacre.

- On May 15, two students are killed by police at Jackson State College.

1971

- The Twenty-sixth Amendment is ratified, reducing the voting age to 18.

- On May 3, the May Day protest temporarily shuts down areas of Washington, DC.

- *Ms.* magazine is founded.

- Designer Yves Saint Laurent launches a controversial fashion line inspired by the 1940s.

1972

- Congress passes the Equal Rights Amendment and sends it to the states for ratification.
- On June 17, a break-in occurs at the offices of the Democratic National Committee at the Watergate Hotel.
- *The Godfather* is released.
- Nixon visits China, reopening relations.
- Swimmer Mark Spitz dominates at the 1972 Olympics.

1973

- In January, the Supreme Court gives its ruling in the *Roe v. Wade* case.
- Congress says there will be no more US military involvement in Vietnam.
- On May 14, the first US space station, Skylab, launches.
- In September, Billie Jean King faces Bobby Riggs in the Battle of the Sexes.
- In October, Syria and Egypt invade Israel, sparking the Yom Kippur War.
- The first call is made on a mobile phone.
- The American League begins to use designated hitters in baseball.

1974

- In March, the oil embargo against the United States is lifted.
- In April, Hank Aaron breaks baseball's home run record.
- On August 8, Nixon resigns and Gerald Ford becomes president.

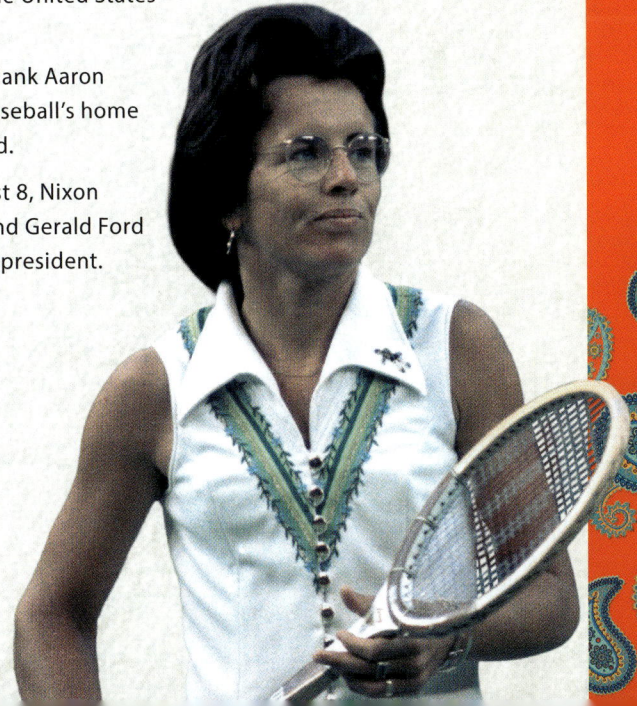

TIMELINE

1975

- In January, the Altair microcomputer is released.
- The home version of the video game *Pong* is released.
- Congress passes the Indochina Migration and Refugee Assistance Act.
- In April, celebrations for the US bicentennial begin.
- Microwave ovens are small enough for home use.
- *Jaws* is released.

1976

- In July, the Apple I computer goes on sale.
- Caitlyn Jenner, who was known at the time as Bruce Jenner, wins the gold medal for the United States in the Olympic decathlon.
- The company JVC introduces the Video Home System (VHS) in Japan.

1978

- Carter invites two foreign leaders, Israeli prime minister Menachem Begin and Egyptian president Anwar Sadat, to Camp David.
- NAVSTAR launches.
- The *Space Invaders* game is released.
- Dave Parker of the Pittsburgh Pirates becomes the first baseball player to earn $1 million a year.
- Speak & Spell by Texas Instruments is the most popular toy.

1977

- Jimmy Carter becomes president.
- The first *Star Wars* movie is released.
- The game *Electronic Football* is introduced.
- President Carter creates the Department of Energy.

1979

- In March, the Three Mile Island nuclear power plant shuts down after a near meltdown.
- In November, the US Embassy in Iran is attacked and staff are taken hostage.
- The TI-99/4 computer is released.

GLOSSARY

abortion

The purposeful ending of a pregnancy.

amnesty

An official pardon granted to people who have been convicted of political offenses or crimes.

census

A government count of the population that also collects data on age, income, and education.

class-action lawsuit

A lawsuit filed by a small group of people on behalf of a larger group to which they belong.

communism

A political system in which the government controls the economy and owns all property.

conscientious objector

Someone who chooses not to participate in military service based on their beliefs about war.

desert

To be absent from the military without leave.

impeachment
A misconduct charge against an elected official.

mainstream
Ideas, attitudes, and activities that are considered normal.

marginalized
Excluded or treated as unimportant or of a lower class.

pardon
To cancel the consequences of a legal offense.

ratification
The act of giving legal approval to an amendment.

shah
A title of the king or ruler of Iran in the past.

summit
A meeting between government leaders.

ADDITIONAL RESOURCES

SELECTED BIBLIOGRAPHY

Lewis, Jerry M., and Thomas R. Hensley. "The May 4 Shootings at Kent State University: The Search for Historical Accuracy." *Kent State University*, 1998, kent.edu. Accessed 11 Jan. 2023.

"Skylab: Science in Space." *Space Race*, n.d., airandspace.si.edu. Accessed 11 Jan. 2023.

Wyckoff, Whitney Blair. "Jackson State: A Tragedy Widely Forgotten." *NPR*, 3 May 2010, npr.org. Accessed 11 Jan. 2023.

FURTHER READINGS

Lane, Laura. *Microsoft*. Abdo, 2019.

Wiles, Deborah. *Kent State*. Scholastic, 2020.

ONLINE RESOURCES

Booklinks
NONFICTION NETWORK
FREE! ONLINE NONFICTION RESOURCES

To learn more about American life in the 1970s, please visit **abdobooklinks.com** or scan this QR code. These links are routinely monitored and updated to provide the most current information available.

MORE INFORMATION

For more information on this subject, contact or visit the following organizations:

Kent State University
800 East Summit St.
Kent, OH 44242
kent.edu
In addition to being a world-class university, Kent State takes its historical role in the Kent State massacre seriously with commemorative markers, annual memorial events, and online articles.

Vietnam Veterans Memorial
5 Henry Bacon Dr. NW
Washington, DC 20245
nps.gov/vive/index.htm
The Vietnam Veterans Memorial honors the soldiers who fought in this conflict. The memorial has a long granite wall etched with the names of the men and women who died in the conflict or are missing.

SOURCE NOTES

CHAPTER 1. KENT STATE

1. Jerry M. Lewis and Thomas R. Hensley. "The May 4 Shootings at Kent State University: The Search for Historical Accuracy." *Kent State University*, n.d., kent.edu. Accessed 1 Aug. 2022.

2. Lewis et al., "The May 4 Shootings at Kent State University."

3. Nicole Speulda. "Youth and War." *Pew Research Center*, 21 Feb. 2006, pewresearch.org. Accessed 1 Aug. 2022.

4. Lewis et al., "The May 4 Shootings at Kent State University."

5. Ronald H. Spector et al. "Vietnam War." *Encyclopedia Britannica*, 13 Mar. 2022, britannica.com. Accessed 1 Aug. 2022.

6. Whitney Blair Wyckoff. "Jackson State: A Tragedy Widely Forgotten." *NPR*, 3 May 2010, npr.org. Accessed 1 Aug. 2022.

7. "Protests and Backlash." *PBS*, n.d., pbs.org. Accessed 1 Aug. 2022.

8. Lewis et al., "The May 4 Shootings at Kent State University."

9. Ben Kesslen. "Kent State Massacre: The Shootings on a College Campus 50 Years Ago Changed the Country." *NBC*, 3 May 2020, nbcnews.com. Accessed 1 Aug. 2022.

CHAPTER 2. AMERICANS OF THE 1970s

1. "1970 Census of Population, Supplementary Report: Race and Urban and Rural Residence of the Population of the United States, by States: 1970." *United States Census Bureau*, Mar. 1972, census.gov. Accessed 1 Aug. 2022.

2. "Top 100 Biggest US Cities in the Year 1970." *Biggest US Cities*, n.d., biggestuscities.com. Accessed 1 Aug. 2022.

3. "Top 100 Biggest US Cities in the Year 1970."

4. "Top 100 Biggest US Cities in the Year 1970."

5. "Top 100 Biggest US Cities in the Year 1970."

6. Geoffrey Migiro. "United States Population by Year." *World Atlas*, 5 Feb. 2020, worldatlas.com. Accessed 1 Aug. 2022.

7. "US Population by Race and Age, 1970-2000." *Research Gate*, n.d., researchgate.net. Accessed 1 Aug. 2022.

8. "U.S. Postwar Immigration Policy." *Council on Foreign Relations*, n.d., cfr.org. Accessed 1 Aug. 2022.

9. "History of Changes to the Minimum Wage Law." *US Department of Labor*, n.d., dol.gov. Accessed 1 Aug. 2022.

10. "Median Family Income Up in 1970." *United States Census Bureau*, 20 May 1971, census.gov. Accessed 1 Aug. 2022.

11. "Poverty Increases by 1.2 Million in 1970." *United States Census Bureau*, 7 May 1971, census.gov. Accessed 1 Aug. 2022.

CHAPTER 3. POLITICS OF THE 1970s

1. Hannah Natanson. "Protestors Shut Down DC Traffic Before. It Helped End the Vietnam War—and Reshaped American Activism." *Washington Post*, 23 Sept. 2019, washingtonpost.com. Accessed 1 Aug. 2022.

2. "When Was the First Earth Day?" *National Ocean Service*, n.d., oceanservice.noaa.gov. Accessed 1 Aug. 2022.

3. Lorraine Boissoneault. "The Cuyahoga River Caught Fire at Least a Dozen Times but No One Cared Until 1969." *Smithsonian*, 19 June 2019, smithsonianmag.com. Accessed 1 Aug. 2022.

CHAPTER 4. WAR AND CONFLICT OF THE 1970s

1. Claire Manisha. "How Young Activists Got 18-Year-Olds the Right to Vote in Record Time." *Smithsonian*, 11 Nov. 2020, smithsonianmag.com. Accessed 1 Aug. 2022.

2. Manisha, "How Young Activists Got 18-Year-Olds the Right to Vote in Record Time."

3. "Significant Events in U.S.–Libyan Relations." *US Department of State*, 2 Sept. 2008, state.gov. Accessed 1 Aug. 2022.

4. "The Iranian Hostage Crisis." *Office of the Historian*, n.d., history.state.gov. Accessed 1 Aug. 2022.

5. "Iran Hostage Crisis." *Encyclopedia Britannica*, 22 Apr. 2022, britannica.com. Accessed 1 Aug. 2022.

CHAPTER 5. SCIENCE AND INVENTION IN THE 1970s

1. "Texas Instruments TI-99." *History of Personal Computing*, n.d., historyofpersonalcomputing.com. Accessed 1 Aug. 2022.

2. "Texas Instruments Model 99/4A Personal Computer." *National Museum of American History*, n.d., americanhistory.si.edu. Accessed 1 Aug. 2022.

3. Rachel Ross. "Who Invented the Microwave Oven?" *Live Science*, 5 Jan. 2017, livescience.com. Accessed 1 Aug. 2022.

4. "Altair 8800 Microcomputer." *National Museum of American History*, n.d., americanhistory.si.edu. Accessed 1 Aug. 2022.

5. "President Carter." *PBS*, n.d., pbs.org. Accessed 1 Aug. 2022.

CHAPTER 6. POP CULTURE OF THE 1970s

1. Priya Ganapati. "June 4, 1977: VHS Comes to America." *Wired*, 4 June 2018, wired.com. Accessed 1 Aug. 2022.

2. Kate Erbland. "How 'Jaws' Forever Changed the Modern Day Blockbuster—and What Today's Examples Could Learn from It." *Indie Wire*, 20 June 2017, indiewire.com. Accessed 1 Aug. 2022.

3. "Star Wars." *Encyclopedia Britannica*, 27 July 2022, britannica.com. Accessed 1 Aug. 2022.

4. "The 13 Most Desired Toys of the 1970s, Year by Year." *Me TV*, 8 Dec. 2016, metv.com. Accessed 1 Aug. 2022.

CHAPTER 7. FASHION OF THE 1970s

1. Landon Peoples. "So, What Is Diane von Furstenberg's Next Big Move?" *Refinery 29*, 31 Dec. 2017, refinery29.com. Accessed 1 Aug. 2022.

CHAPTER 8. SPORTS OF THE 1970s

1. Joe Reedy. "A Look at the Seminal Broadcasting Moves That Defined the NFL." *AP News*, 24 Aug. 2019, apnews.com. Accessed 1 Aug. 2022.

2. Fred Mitchell. "Flashback: Bobby Hull Leaving the Blackhawks for the WHA." *Chicago Tribune*, 18 July 2015, chicagotribune.com. Accessed 1 Aug. 2022.

3. Murray Crass. "Park Signs $5 Million Contract." *New York Times*, 27 Jan. 1979, nytimes.com. Accessed 1 Aug. 2022.

4. "Title IX." *Encyclopedia Britannica*, 16 June 2022, britannica.com. Accessed 1 Aug. 2022.

5. "Women's Tennis Association." *Billie Jean King*, n.d., billiejeanking.com. Accessed 1 Aug. 2022.

6. "Battle of the Sexes." *Billie Jean King*, n.d., billiejeanking.com. Accessed 1 Aug. 2022.

7. "Battle of the Sexes."

8. "Munich Massacre." *Encyclopedia Britannica*, 29 Aug. 2021, britannica.com. Accessed 1 Aug. 2022.

CHAPTER 9. THE LEGACY OF THE 1970s

1. Candice Norwood. "How New Gen Z Voters Could Shape the Election." *PBS News Hour*, 31 Oct. 2020, pbs.org. Accessed 1 Aug. 2022.

2. "'Title IX,' or Why the Americans Have Some of the Best Female Football Players in the World." *Olympics*, 7 July 2019, olympics.com. Accessed 1 Aug. 2022.

3. "Male vs Female Professional Sports Salary Comparison." *Adelphi University*, n.d., adelphi.edu. Accessed 1 Aug. 2022.

4. Melissa Leon. "How 'Star Wars' Revolutionized the Toy Industry." *Daily Beast*, 6 Jan. 2018, thedailybeast.com. Accessed 1 Aug. 2022.

INDEX

ABOUT THE AUTHOR

SUE BRADFORD EDWARDS

Sue Bradford Edwards and her husband grew up in the 1970s as fans of *Star Wars* and *Star Trek*, wearing bell-bottoms and even granny-square vests. Edwards is the author of 22 other titles from Abdo, including *Black Lives Matter*, *Coronavirus: The COVID-19 Pandemic*, *The Impeachment of Donald Trump*, *The Dakota Access Pipeline*, and *The Zika Virus*.

ABOUT THE CONSULTANT

BENJAMIN C. WATERHOUSE

Benjamin C. Waterhouse is a professor of history at the University of North Carolina at Chapel Hill, where he teaches courses on modern US politics, business, and society, including a class on the United States in the 1970s. His books focus on US political and business history, with a particular focus on the period since the 1960s. He holds a bachelor's degree from Princeton University and a PhD from Harvard University.